STEPFAMILIES—
LIVING IN CHRISTIAN HARMONY

STEPFAMILIES
LIVING IN CHRISTIAN HARMONY

BOBBIE REED

Publishing House
St. Louis

Acknowledgments

The "Social Readjustment Scale" is a reprint from the Journal of Psychosomatic Research, 11:213—8, by T. H. Holmes and R. H. Rahe. Copyright © 1967, Pergamon Press, Ltd. Used by permission of the author.

The "General Adaptation Syndrome," Figure 3—2, is from the book Stress Without Distress, by Hans Selye, M.D. Copyright © 1974 by Hans Selye, M. D. Reprinted by permission of J. B. Lippincott Company.

The "Etiology Chart," Figure 3—3, is from the soon-to-be-published book Stress—The Challenge of Understanding, The Art of Coping, by James R. Walt, Psy. D. Used by permission of the author.

Poem "Daddy's House," by Leilani Cottingham Collins. Used by permission of the author.

"The Age of Becoming," by Dorothy Williams. Used by permission of the author.

Library of Congress Cataloging in Publication Data

Reed, Bobbie.
     Stepfamilies, living in Christian harmony.

     Bibliography: p. 139
     1. Family—Religious life. I. Title.
BV4526.2.R43   248'.4   79-20168
ISBN 0-570-03798-0

To my sons,
Jonathan and Michael,
through whom I gained personal knowledge
of steprelationships;

and

To Leilani and Jim,
whose constant love for one another
demonstrates that stepfamilies can work,
even under the most adverse
circumstances.

Contents

Power, Who's Got the Power? . . . I Need You . . .
Who's Who . . . The Grass Is Always Greener . . .
Jesus Was a Stepchild

Introduction
≈ᢧ ᡦᢛ

One out of every four children in America have one or more stepparents.

—Stepparents who have never had children of their own.

—Stepparents whose children live with their other parents.

—Stepparents whose children share their home.

—Stepparents whose children are grown up and have homes of their own.

Stepfamilies working at learning to live together. Because of the historically negative connotation of the word "step," alternative terms are suggested by various contemporary writers:

—"synergistic family"

—"blended family"

—"reconstituted family"

—"poly-" (instead of "step" prefix)

—"---by marriage" (for example, "mother by marriage" or "son by marriage")

However, the old familiar word "step" is still the term of prefix most frequently used to identify relationships in families where the children are the biological offspring of only one of the spouses.

Stepfamilies Differ from Biological Families

In spite of the fact that on the surface stepfamilies resemble biological families (there's Mom, Dad, and children), significant differences exist.

One (or both) of the spouses become(s) an instant parent to the child(ren) of the new mate. But the instant parent is not presented with a tiny infant, which is a precious reminder of moments of shared love. Instead the child represents the spouse's previous intimate relationship with someone else.

And, the child comes readymade, complete with ideas, values, opinions, preferences, and living habits. Seldom are these totally compatible with the expectations of the new stepparent. The underlying affinity that is built over the years between a natural parent and a biological offspring is missing in steprelationships.

Stepfamilies also differ from biological families in that the children are usually shared with the other natural parents. Visitation arrangements with the noncustodial parent vary from family to family, and many children living in steprelationships actually have two homes—a situation they often adjust to better than do their parents.

Perhaps the greatest difference between stepfamilies and biological families is the configuration of the "nuclear family." In biological families, Mom, Dad, and the children form the "nuclear family." Other relatives (grandparents, aunts, uncles, cousins, in-laws) take their place around the family as if in concentric circles of decreasing intimacy. In stepfamilies, however, the "nuclear family" seems to include the couple, the children, and the other natural parent(s) of the children! For in spite of the fact that there are ex-spouses, these are not ex-parents! And so, whether they intrude in person by their correspondence or calls, or in the memories of the children, their presence and influence are very real.

Because of these additional members (outsiders who are not really outsiders), stepfamilies are subjected to pressures, frustrations, and demands that no biological family experiences. For years sociologists, psychologists, and other professionals have promulgated principles for effective one-on-one relationships and child rearing. Most of the time we recognize what we're doing right and what we're doing wrong in these areas. But only recently have the experts started writing about the intricacies of steprelationships. Few of us are completely prepared for the day-to-day realities.

The Challenges

There are no problems—only challenges!

A problem is something that is standing between you and your objective. A challenge is something you overcome on your way to your objective. There are challenges in steprelationships:

hidden and open resentments, financial demands, time and schedule conflicts, expectations, communications, and legal involvements.

Contrary to glowing expectations and bright hopes, the everyday realities are often harsh. And yet stepfamilies can be successful if each member recognizes that the relationships are fragile and need to be handled with prayer.

There has yet to be written a book which gives the answer! At best, practical suggestions are offered in the spirit of sharing what others have learned through experience. This book is no exception. The research included:

—interviews with people in steprelationships (some are named below, others requested anonymity);

—interviews with child, family, and marriage counselors;

—interviews with pastors and church leaders;

—interviews with divorce and custody lawyers;

—a review of current literature on the subject;

—my own experiences in steprelationships.

In grateful recognition of their contributions of time and personal sharing, I wish to thank the following people:

Richard Baker, Licensed Clinical Social Worker

Paul Bellwood, Minister of Singles, First Baptist Church of Fair Oaks, California

Stephen Brown, Pastor, Emmanuel Baptist Church, Sacramento, California

Paul J. Christianssen, Headmaster, St. Michael's Episcopal Day School

James Collins, Governmental Program Analyst, California State Department of Mental Health

Leilani Cottingham Collins, Assistant Press Officer, California State Department of Mental Health

Duane Flores-Goff

Lynne Goutermont

Russell and Carroll Hess

Elaine Juliusson, Consultant, Vocational Rehabilitation Counselor

Gerald Kassow, Attorney at Law

Pamela King, MSW, Social Worker and Legal Advocate, Sacramento Legal Aid Society, Domestic Relations Unit

Barrie Lamonte, PSW, Clinical Social Worker

Brinkley A. Long, Director of Family Court Services
Barbara McCallum, Attorney at Law
Debbie Meyer
Virginia Mueller, Attorney at Law
Bud and Kathy Pearson, Ministers to Single Adults, Garden Grove Community Church
Jonathan Reed
Michael Reed
Betty Russell, Clinical Social Worker
Thomas L. Russell, MSW, Licensed Clinical Social Worker
Elaine Shelton
Kenneth Slavney, ACSW, Children's Mental Health Programs Specialist, California State Department of Mental Health
Paul A. Smith, Training Consultant, California State Department of Developmental Services
Emily Visher, President, Stepfamily Foundation, Palo Alto, California
Dottie Williams, Personnel Manager, Legislative Counsel of California
Patricia Williams

Part One:
Understanding Steprelationships

Chapter One
Considering That Second Walk Down the Aisle

<d ̊ ß>

A second chance at love, courtship, and marriage! A whole, new start! Fantastic! And it's happening to you! You love each other. Have so much fun together. Like the same things. Never disagree.

Do you sometimes feel that it's too good to be true? It may be! Over 1.3 million people a year in the United States are discovering that princes on white horses and beautiful princesses live happily ever after only in fairy tales. Undaunted by this discovery, 80 percent of those people remarry after their divorces. The high rate of second divorces suggests that many who remarry do so with their fairy tale fantasies intact, at least until reality becomes impossible to ignore. The cycle starts again: divorce, remarriage, divorce, remarriage.

Break the Failure Cycle

Aaron, a writer, had just purchased a new typewriter—an IBM Selectric. Thrilled with his new toy, he immediately sat down to type a new article. After completing a couple of pages he read what he had typed. Something was terribly wrong! At least every tenth word was gibberish. Bitterly disappointed that his prized possession was imperfect, he returned the typewriter to the store, taking along the typed page as proof that the machine was useless.

The manager called the repairman to the front of the store so Aaron could explain the problem. With scarcely a glance at the typed evidence, the repairman reached for a repair slip and quietly said ". . . m-m-m. It's been malselecting, huh? You can pick it up in three days. OK?"

Right there in the middle of a business machine show-room, Aaron had a flash of insight about his own, personal life. Only the night before he had been struggling with depression over his seeming inability to develop relationships which worked. He had been divorced twice, and now his latest girl friend had just broken off with him. Last night's depression and self-doubts had focused on the question, "What am I doing wrong?"

"Malselecting," the salesman had said in a quiet voice. But the word seemed to flash in Aaron's mind with the brilliant intensity of a neon sign. "Malselecting! That's what I've been doing! I've been selecting the women whose characteristics are incompatible with my own needs in a relationship!" he thought.

Aaron had always been attracted to self-sufficient, independent, capable women who had successful careers of their own, without verifying that those women also had the other qualities he wanted (affection, love, sharing, giving). Each had her own circle of friends and personal interests apart from those shared with Aaron. None of the women in his life had been interested enough in building a real marriage to invest her time or herself. The logical end to a conflict between the other aspects of their lives and their marriage was that the relationship was canceled.

Aaron shared recently, "I've been taking a look at my values and expectations. I still find independent, strong, capable women exciting. But I've also found that there are other manifestations of these qualities that I hadn't noticed complete-ly before. I've seen emotional strength in women who are not only surviving; but they are actually conquering experiences from which the traditionally 'strong' woman (vocal, forceful, ambitious) would walk away. I've seen capability at the office matched by the ability to be a giving, loving person in a difficult relationship—sometimes both of these in the same person. And an avid interest in some sport, hobby, or career can bring people together instead of pushing them apart, if the interest is shared.

"I feel as if I've been given the key to the most complex mystery of my life!" Aaron concludes.

Aaron is breaking his failure cycle!

Family and marriage counselors caution us that unless people take time and make a conscious effort to effect positive life changes between marriages they will probably repeat their previous mistakes. Choose the same type of mate. Relate the same way. Fail again. If you are considering remarriage, read this chapter carefully. If you have already remarried, use this chapter to identify issues that you and your mate have yet to resolve together, and start breaking your failure cycles, right now.

Know Yourself

During marriage a couple forms a joint identity which influences each of the individual's self-images. When the marriage ends, each person must reevaluate and reestablish his personal identity and self-image, apart from the marriage relationship. A person whose personal identity is confused, incomplete, or still intertwined with a previous relationship is not ready for a new marriage. He is not yet whole.

Individual wholeness is essential to a successful alliance between two people. Marriage should not be the uniting of two broken halves but the joining of two whole people to form a strong union. Since none of us is perfect, we do tend to admire and be attracted to strengths in others in those areas in which we feel ourselves to be weak. But this attraction should not result in an overdependency on the spouse for our basic identity.

Therefore, a person who is still grieving over the loss of a spouse, or smarting with bitterness and resentment against an ex-spouse, needs more time for healing before remarriage.

If marriage is one of the most difficult partnerships to make successful, remarriage with its innumerable complications and unexpected problems (especially when children are involved) is even more of a challenge. So if you're contemplating entering a stepfamily relationship, be sure that you know yourself to be ready.

That means—

1. Being in a good, spiritual space

Before we can truly succeed in a human relationship, we must have a right relationship with our Lord. When we are self-centered, we find that we are concerned with getting our own ways, often unforgiving, easily angered, and sometimes less than loving. Only when He is at the center of our lives can we keep things in a proper perspective and love one another freely.

Keeping our relationship with God in good working order requires a regular time for personal worship and communion with Him—talking alone with God, meditating on His Word, living by the principles in His Word, succeeding at all we do—that's the sequence He promised. (See Joshua 1:7-9, Psalm 1:1-3, Matthew 6:33.)

2. Being in a good, intellectual space

As unemotionally as possible we must carefully analyze our previous experiences with relationships and/or marriage in an attempt to identify what worked and why, as well as what went wrong and why. This self-analysis forms the basis of a personal growth plan for preparing ourselves for future relationships. We need to review our expectations of a relationship and of a spouse to ensure that our fantasies have been replaced by realistic possibilities. We must recognize that we (and our future spouses) will make mistakes, but we are prepared to be slow to anger and quick to forgive. These are signs of being in a good, intellectual space for remarriage. One caution remains: we should not be under extreme intellectual stress (for example, finals week of our graduate studies, or studying for the bar exam) at the time of our remarriage, or we will have insufficient mental energy to devote to the new relationship.

3. Being in a good, emotional space

We shouldn't be at either extreme of the "moodmeter." A person who is very depressed, or who is naively and deliriously oblivious to any suggestion of reality is not yet ready for a permanent, new relationship. Being emotionally balanced is essential. It involves forgiveness of ourselves, our ex-spouses, and our children for any past failures to meet our expectations or to minister to our needs. It means being in touch with and accepting our feelings, and assuming the responsibility for our own happiness and emotional well-being.

Each partner in the remarriage needs to be in a good place, spiritually, intellectually, and emotionally. Each must be whole. One individual cannot bear the responsibility for both.

"I think Jack probably needs some time to get used to not being married to Grace." Cindy said. "But he wants us to get married as soon as his divorce is final. I don't want to lose him, so I'm going along with his plans. Maybe it will be OK."

Maybe it will.

Maybe it won't!

Take time to know yourself before you remarry.

Know What You Want!

"It's time to rethink marriage when thinking remarriage," cautions Robert P. Merkle, a marriage, family, and child counselor.

Unrealistic expectations are the deadliest enemies of a relationship. Do you and your future spouse know what you are expecting from each other, from the marriage, and from the children? Are you realistic? Take a look at the realities. Talk to friends who are, or have been, involved in stepfamilies to get different perspectives of the challenges and the rewards.

As you identify your expectations, share them with your future spouse. Openly discuss your dreams and desires, your hopes and fears. Expressing an expectation of your future spouse doesn't guarantee that your expectation will be met! But as you discuss your wants, your partner will have the choice of fulfilling your "demand" or of understanding your disappointment when the "demand" is not met. The dialog also serves as a way of clarifying demands and of eliminating those expectations that are unrealistic. Your mate may not agree with your assumption that your concepts are rational, logical, or even desirable! That's OK! It's through this type of sharing that you come to know your future spouse on an intellectually and emotionally intimate level. As you confront each other in love, you grow both as individuals and as a couple.

Unrealistic expectations are born of our dreams of a perfect marriage whose perpetual harmony is a legend in its own time! Or perhaps these expectations come from a desperate need to find a specific perfection that we feel is vital to our happiness. Read through the following partial list of typical **unrealistic demands** as you check your own hopes.

    1. Marriage—
        a. Can be perfect.
        b. Is always better than single.
        c. Means never wishing I were single again.
        d. Means less responsibility and more freedom.

    e. Means togetherness that is always rewarding.
    f. Can't be hurt by conflicting schedules, sharing bathrooms, or differing values if it is a good relationship.
    g. Is never lonely.
    h. Will make me feel complete.
    i. Is all I'll ever want.

2. My future spouse—
    a. Will always give me space to be alone and grow as an individual.
    b. Will make me happy.
    c. Will always be there for me (emotionally, physically, spiritually) when I need him/her most.
    d. Won't have expections of me which will infringe on my own personal freedoms.
    e. Will love my children as his/her own.
    f. Will have children whom I will instantly find lovable.
    g. Will agree with my desire to have (or not have) more children.
    h. Will agree with my values, beliefs, discipline methods, and goals.
    i. Will have been used to the same life-style as I have.
    j. Will be a perfect mate.
    k. Will not have any serious problems in life (personal, financial, social, psychological, physical, or emotional).
    l. Will not change his/her expectations of me.
    m. Will always have a sense of humor and see the funny side of sticky situations.

3. I—
    a. Will be the perfect mate.
    b. Will make my spouse happy.
    c. Will be a super stepparent.
    d. Will instantly love my mate's children.
    e. Won't be resented by my mate's ex-spouse, children, family, or friends.
    f. Will never long for the familiar problems of singlehood instead of the challenges of stepkinship.
    g. Will never fail.
    h. Will do my best, and it will be enough.

i. Will never feel pushed, excluded, ignored, imposed upon, tired, resentful, or angry.
j. Will never repeat past mistakes.
k. Know enough to avoid mistakes and problems.
l. Will not change my expectations of my spouse and family.
m. Will always have a sense of humor and see the funny side of sticky situations.
n. Will have no problem living in the same house or community as did my mate and the ex-spouse.
o. Will have no problem living in the same community as my mate's ex-spouse does now.

4. The children—
a. Will at once get along with (obey, respect, like, or love) their new stepparent.
b. Will not feel threatened by the remarriage of one of their parents.
c. Will not act out.
d. Will never need professional counseling to adjust to the new marriage.
e. Will not fail to adjust.
f. Will never be unkind, thoughtless, rude, disobedient, or exasperating.
g. Will accept, and not test, the limits you and your mate set down.
h. Will not need time alone with their parent apart from the new stepparent.
i. Are only part of the family equation if they have their permanent home with you.
j. Will never come to live with you if yours is the noncustodial home.
k. Could never come between you and your mate.
l. Will never deliberately cause trouble.
m. Will always have a sense of humor and see the funny side of sticky situations.
n. Of the opposite sex from mine will not be a problem to me.
o. With special challenges (physical disabilities or emotional distrubances) are no problem.
p. Will be easy to adjust to, even if I've never had

children of my own.
5. God—
    a. Promises instant success.
    b. Will make both me and my spouse better people, capable of a perfect union.
    c. Will stop us from making mistakes.
    d. Will protect us from making unwise choices.
    e. Will take the responsibility for making me happy.
    f. Will agree with my priorities, timing, methods, and plans for my marriage.
    g. Will side with me when my mate and I disagree.
    h. Loves me so much He won't make me suffer the consequences of my unwise choices.
    i. Doesn't want to be involved in the details of my daily live.
6. The ex-spouses—
    a. Will never be resentful, jealous, or spiteful.
    b. Could never cause trouble between my mate and me.
    c. Will not take advantage of me.
    d. Will not intrude on my marriage (through financial demands, memories, the children, or requests for help).

Well! How did your own expectations survive the checklist? Do you and your future spouse have a fairly realistic view of the coalition you are forming? The bottom line is that you both must be flexible enough to work through conflicts of needs, values, and expectations if you are to succeed.

Resolving conflicts facilitates the process of getting to know your future spouse. You become friends as well as lovers in your marriage. You may want to take a course in family relations or even go for extensive premarital counseling. At least you will want to work through a couple of good books such as:

Wes Roberts and Norman Wright, Before You Say I Do, (Irvine, CA: Harvest House Publishers, 1978) or John Powell, The Secret of Staying in Love (Niles, IL: Argus Communications, 1974).

As you plan your marriage, be realistic in your expectations of the children involved. While children need not be intimately included in a parent's experimental dating, they should be included in the relationship once marriage plans are underway. Professional counselors disagree regarding whether children should be asked for permission or simply informed of the upcoming marriage. Those who advocate asking claim that by this act you show the child that he is important to you, and you therefore win his cooperation. Those who suggest telling the children have at least one strong argument on their side—unless you plan to call off your wedding if the child says no, you are only being dishonest by pretending to obtain permission. Asking a child to decide your future places too heavy a burden on him, since he is likely to have strongly conflicting feelings about the remarriage of his parent. A child can feel important by being involved in planning for the remarriage, without being asked for permission to remarry in order to feel included in the excitement and love.

During the premarital interaction, children need to experience their future stepparent as he or she really is. If you are the prospective new parent, be honest in expressing your feelings, your needs, and desires. Being otherwise (too kind, too cooperative, too unassuming) allows children to form unrealistic expectations of you.

One of the recommendations for a successful remarriage that was mentioned by nearly every couple and professional interviewed was to develop a ready sense of humor. Learn to laugh in the midst of the most bizarre or difficult situations. Don't take life or yourself too seriously. Don't let things become a matter of life and death—you may lose! Learn to care without coming unglued! Learn to relax under stress. Learn to flow with life without always fighting to go upstream.

Remember, you can win!

Plan Ahead

"Bill and I have problems in solving mutual problems, because we're so different in our approaches. But we'll work things out after we're married," Karen said lightly, with a wave of her hand as if brushing aside fictitious barriers.

Of course, you can work most things out, if you plan ahead! Management consultants today emphasize the importance of planning. A manager who only spends 10 percent of his time in planning activities will find that up to 75 percent of his time is spent responding to crises for which he had no contingency plans. On the other hand, a manager who spends a significant percent of his time developing effective short-range, long-range, and contingency plans has few instances of unanticipated problems. Production proceeds smoothly, and the business is usually successful.

This same principle applies to a couple planning marriage. The less they plan ahead, the more significant the problems. The more they plan, the fewer the crises.

One can make detailed plans for most aspects of the future relationship. For example:

1. Family spiritual life
   —What church to attend;
   —Which services to attend regularly;
   —What church activities to participate in;
   —When to have family worship;
   —When to have personal devotions.
2. House rules
   —Who does what chores?
   —Curfew and bedtimes;
   —When homework is to be completed.
   —Who selects which television programs to watch?
   —Who gets what privileges and when?
   —Mealtimes;
   —Who gets to use the telephone; for how long?
3. Specific standards for behavior
   —Courtesies required!
   —Absolute "don'ts"!
   —Required "do's"!
   —Specific consequences for inappropriate behaviors (discipline);
   —Specific rewards for acceptable, and outstanding, behaviors.
4. Problem solving
   —Who is included?
   —What methods will be used (group discussion, family council, unilateral parental mandates, debates, etc.)?
   —How to resolve conflicts of needs;
   —How to resolve conflicts of wants;

—How to creatively confront;
—How to teach children problem-solving skills.
5. Personal growth
    —How to give each family member room to develop as an individual;
    —How to ensure interaction between various family members;
    —How to ensure each family member privacy when needed;
    —How to give each family member the freedom to try, to risk, to succeed, or to fail.
6. Communications
    —How to keep the channels open;
    —When to listen instead of talking;
    —How to encourage openness in sharing;
    —How to express feelings;
    —How to accept the feelings expressed by someone else;
    —How to show love and respect one for another.

The list could be endless! And sooner or later you and your spouse will have to plan how to handle each of these and many other situations. Sooner might make a significant difference in your marriage. Later might be too late to save the relationship.

Count the Cost

Show me a three-week-old German Shepherd puppy, and my response is predictable. I feel an incredibly powerful rush of protective affection bringing unexplainable tears to my eyes. Of their own volition my arms reach out to take the puppy. I must hold it, cuddle it, stroke its soft furry coat. More than anything else in the world at that moment, I want that dog!

Then reality intervenes: I remember that if I take the puppy home, he becomes my responsibility. And I know that this precious moment of holding this irresistible puppy won't last forever. Little puppies grow into big dogs who aren't always cuddly, sweet, and adorable. I have no room in my home for a big dog. I don't want to go through the housebreaking training, or to have my possessions broken by a boisterous, growing puppy, however cute he may be. I don't make a good dog owner.

Ever so reluctantly I force myself to put the puppy back with his mother and walk away. A little part of me seems to die, yet I know I've made the right decision.

Before making commitments, we need to carefully count the cost to be sure we are willing to pay the price. Sometimes the cost is much too high and the investment unwise. Yet, it's far easier to walk away from a little puppy we think we want than to let go of a bad relationship. If we took time to honestly look at the long-range outcome of a bad relationship, we might see that there are irreconcilable differences which might later break up the marriage, and we might think twice before forging ahead. By counting the cost we can avoid those relationships which are doomed to failure and remain available for a relationship which has every chance to succeed.

Unfortunately, there are no guarantees when it comes to relationships. So be sure when contemplating remarriage that you have broken the failure cycle and won't be repeating the problems you may have had in a previous marriage. Get in touch with yourself so that you are clear about what you bring to the relationship, what you want out of the union, and what you are willing to invest in the marriage. And remember God's promises—in His strength you can succeed. That second walk down the aisle doesn't have to mean a second walk out of a divorce court.

Chapter Two
Discussing the Forbidden
Topic—Money

~~~

"I never thought money would be an important issue in any relationship," Linda shares solemnly. "I'm not a materialistic person. But, what with assuming the debts from Ken's previous marriage, paying the attorney and psychiatric examination fees for our custody suit, making child and spousal support payments to Ken's ex-wife, as well as paying for numerous other expenses (such as dental and medical bills) for the kids, we've paid out over $15,000 this year.

"Ken and I both have good jobs, but we can't afford to keep paying out at the rate we have been. Although I hate to admit it—now that we can't even afford to go out to McDonald's for a hamburger if we want to—I resent the money we are spending as a result of Ken's previous marriage!"

Linda and Ken's story is not that unusual. Often the previous marriage results in financial demands on the new marriage. When the demands are extreme, the impact can be devastating, and only a very strong relationship can survive.

Many people are uncomfortable discussing personal finances. Asking questions about the financial status of a future mate seems to violate personal privacy. Being open about one's own budget may leave the door open for criticism of individual money management habits. Therefore, all too often, money is the one subject the couple doesn't discuss before remarriage. The resultant horror stories are not surprising.

—A man marries a woman who does not have a job outside the home, yet she has been living luxuriously in a nice apartment. He assumes she is free of financial worries. After they are married, he discovers that her primary income had been spousal support from her ex-husband and that the income stopped when she remarried.

—A woman marries a man who has an excellent job and lives modestly. She assumes that he must be the type to save a substantial portion of his paycheck. Later she discovers that 75 percent of his take-home pay is being spent on debts from his previous marriage and on child and spousal support. (NOTE: Divorce courts are usually fair about dividing up assets and liabilities between the husband and wife. Yet, often the party wanting out of the marriage volunteers to take the debts and leave the assets. Attorneys cite several reasons for this: guilt, a feeling that the ex-spouse can't, or won't, make the payments and a desire to speed up the divorce process.)

—A woman marries a man who has been taking her out to eat several times a week and has been buying her expensive gifts. She discovers that in order to do that he has not kept up payments on the household accounts. She also finds out that this is his usual spending style and that he doesn't mind being just one step ahead of the creditors.

—A man marries a woman who seems to be managing her finances quite well. Then she tells him that she has been borrowing from every friend or relative who would loan her money, had refinanced her house, and had borrowed to the credit limit from every lending source she knew. She was thousands of dollars in debt and would be repaying money for years.

There were many other stories people shared. Everyone agreed that openness before marriage would have been preferable to the shock of reality after the wedding. Only a few people admitted that they might have avoided the marriage had they known the facts.

What about the people who had the financial problems? When asked why they didn't confide in their future spouses, they predominantly agreed that they hadn't foreseen finances as a major problem, and would have answered any direct questions posed by their future mates!

Identify Your Resources
Before you can plan a budget which is appropriate for you and your future spouse, you have to determine your available

resources and your existing liabilities. Each of you should do an individual financial assessment before you attempt to consolidate resources.

1. Determine your individual income.

List all sources of income which you receive, the amount and frequency of payments. Be sure to include: your primary job; any part-time work (teaching, writing, consulting, baby-sitting); spousal or child-support payments; annual dividends on investments; or interest derived from savings.

2. Determine your basic expenses.

Make a list of all of your expenses for a normal month. The following list is an example:

Item	Amount of monthly payment
Rent or mortage	$
Electricity	
Gas (house)	
Water	
Sewage	
Refuse service	
Telephone	
Food	
Repairs	
Gasoline (car)	
Car repair and maintenance (tires, etc.)	
Insurance	
Medical	
Dental	
Life	
Car	
Fire and theft	
Other	
Medical bills	
Drugs	
Doctor's office visits	
Dental appointments	
Education	
Tuition	
Books, supplies	

Item	Amount of monthly payment
Clothing	$
Purchase	
Laundry, dry cleaning	
Donations	
Church	
Other	
Dues	
Union	
Associations or clubs	
Savings	
Credit Union	
Bank	
Savings bonds	
Other	
Support payments	
Child	
Spousal	
Personal spending	
Meals/snack at work	
Eating out	
Beauty/barber shop	
Entertainment	
Vacation	
Children's allowances	
Pet bills	
(Vet. bills, grooming, etc.)	
Charge accounts	
(List by name)	
Loan repayments	
(List by source)	
Miscellaneous	
Average Total Monthly Expenditures	$

Subtract your average monthly expenditures from your monthly income to determine if you are living within your resources or not.

3. List your assets and liabilities.
Next make a list of your assets with the estimated value of

each. Assets include your possessions, your savings, your retirement fund, savings bonds, stock certificates, and moneys owed you.

Finally, list your total indebtedness, including: first and second mortgages, charge accounts, installment plan purchases, outstanding loans, and credit union accounts.

When you have completed the assessment, share what you have written with your partner. Refrain from making value judgements about how your partner has been managing money.

Evaluate Your Life-Style

After you have identified your joint resources and liabilities, you and your future mate are ready to evaluate the life-style you are planning together. Given your income and fixed expenses, will you be able to afford what you are planning?

1. Set goals

Discuss your individual and joint financial goals. Share what you would like to achieve financially.
—Buy a home?
—Pay off a mortgage?
—Own your own business?
—Get out of debt?
—Start or build a savings account?
—Buy a new car?
—Buy a recreation vehicle?
—Buy a boat?
—Travel?

Discuss your desires openly and honestly. If you can agree on goals, then set the date for reaching those goals.

2. Discuss options.

Once you have set financial goals, evaluate your current income and expenditures. Are there an expesnes you might cut back on for a limited amount of time in order to reach your goals more quickly? Are there ways to augment your income temporarily? Be careful, however, about taking on a second job. The extra income comes in handy, but the time spent away from your spouse and family may not be worth the extra money. Also, the strain of the longer working hours may result in a person being too tired to contribute personal involvement to the relationship.

3. Develop a budget.

The next step is to develop a workable budget for the two of you. Be sure to allow at least a slim cushion for unexpected expenses. You don't want every emergency to completely destroy your budget. Also allow yourselves at least a little something extra each month to make the austerity of your budget bearable. You might go out to eat in a nice restaurant once a month. Or if you are a "junk food addict," go to McDonald's twice a month. Only you can decide what will meet your needs. But remember, if you deprive yourself totally, you probably won't be willing to stay on your budget long enough to reach your goals.

Decide what you will do with any leftover money at the end of the month.

—Save it for next month's emergency.

—Make an extra charge account payment.

—Splurge on something special
   (eat out, buy clothes, go to the theater).

—Deposit it in your savings account.

4. Stick to your budget.

"I can write terrific budgets, but I never stick to them," Helen confessed. Perhaps you too have that problem. Here are a few hints.

—Pray together as you develop your budget asking God to give you both wisdom in planning as well as strength to follow through on your plan. Commit your spending habits to God.

—Select a savings and loan or bank that makes it easy for you to save but difficult to withdraw early from your account.

—Consider having your bank automatically transfer a set amount from your checking account to your savings account each month. Or save by payroll deduction. In this way you don't have a monthly choice about whether or not to save money.

—Don't carry extra cash and make it easy for yourself to purchase unnecessary items.

—Don't go to a sale unless a specific item you have included in the budget is on sale.

—Don't go shopping unless you are seeking a specific

budgeted item, and then buy only that one item.

—Save your change. It adds up.

—When you have made the last payments on a loan or charge account, continue "spending" that amount by either depositing it in your savings account or by making extra payments on other accounts.

—Once you have deposited money into a savings account, consider it spent. Do not think of it as available to you should you decide to impulsively change your goals. This does not meant that you cannot withdraw money in case of a real emergency, but be sure it is an emergency.

—Don't change your goals without at least as much consideration as you gave the original goal-setting process.

Reaching your financial goals is a possibility if you develop a realistic budget and follow your plan.

Consider Your Attitudes

Having sufficient income to cover the usual expenses may not be a problem. A couple can still get into financial difficulties if one or both of the partners are poor stewards of the resources that God has given them. If one or more of the following statements is true for you, perhaps you should reconsider your attitudes about your finances.

1. I spend money to compensate for negative moods and feelings (depression, anxiety, fear, anger). The more intense the feeling, the more I spend.

2. I use money to get even with others. If my spouse disappoints me, I destroy the budget with a large, unbudgeted purchase.

3. I consider tithing to be living "under the law." I just give to the Lord when I have some money left over.

4. I use money to reward myself. If I achieve a goal, I give myself an expensive present even if I can't afford it.

5. I like to give expensive gifts even if I can't afford it.

6. I enjoy being generous. I often buy lunch for my co-workers. I don't understand why my spouse resents this.

7. I earn it; I'm entitled to enjoy it. I live up to my income and don't feel a need to save.

8. I spend money as fast as I earn it. "Money burns a hole in my pocket."

9. I feel that living on a budget is restrictive. I just earn it and spend it.

10. I never balance my checkbook. Why bother? If I'm overdrawn, the bank will let me know.

Discussing your attitudes about money and your spending habits is a significant must for complete openness in your marriage. Decide ahead of time, if you will have joint checking and saving accounts, who will be repsonsible for which expenses and who will assume the "bookkeeping" duties for the marriage. If there is significant disagreement on financial matters between you and your future spouse, consider professional counseling or working through a good book. Here are two suggestions:

Rich Yohn, God's Answer to Financial Problems (Irvine, CA: Harvest House Publishers, 1978)

Dale Galloway, There Is a Solution to Your Money Problems (Glendale, CA: Regal Books, 1976)

Don't take a chance on letting financial disagreements ruin your marriage. Instead, give God priority in your life— including your pocketbook! Strive to use your resources for the enhancement of your family life and for the glory of God.

Chapter Three
Avoiding the End
of Your Rope

&ej ȝ꙽

"If one more thing goes wrong, I'm going to go stark, raving mad!"

"I'm at the end of my rope!"

"I just can't cope any longer!"

Do these statements sound familiar? Most of us have made similar comments at various times in our lives, signaling that we are experiencing stress overload. Effectively coping with extreme or constant stress has come to be almost an absolute requirement in today's hurry-scurry world. Yet before we can cope, we must first understand stress itself.

What Is Stress?

People nod knowingly when a co-worker is hospitalized after a heart attack and comment among themselves that their colleague had been under a lot of stress lately. People who are constantly and intensely involved in several high pressure activities are often warned by friends that if they don't slow down or learn to relax, the stress will kill them. Tension headaches are attributed to stress. And executives admit to being under stress when faced with too many demands and too few resources.

While all of these concepts are not totally erroneous, they are based on the premise that stress is an external force over which the individual has little control. A look at the clinical definition of stress and an investigation of research findings reveal the surprising truth that stress is actually the body's internal response to external changes.

Change is a fact of life. Our world is in a constant state of change. Political liasons are formed and broken in quick succession. Revolutions give birth to new revolutions. Nothing seems stable.

Our society is perhaps the most changeable in the world. New technology and research seems to affect our lives daily, in one way or another. A new product appears on the supermarket shelves. Labels shout "new, improved" at the customers. New products are taken off shelves because they have been found to cause cancer in rats and are therefore potentially dangerous to our health.

Each year thousands of laws are passed, regulations adopted, and court decisions made that impact our daily lives.

Our social world changes. Close friends move away. A co-worker is promoted. A neighbor dies. The ideal marriage ends in the divorce court. Our children attend junior high school where sex and drugs are simple realities.

Some changes are career related. We transfer, are promoted, or change jobs. New discoveries in our professional discipline quickly obsolete the skills we learned in the past. We must keep abreast.

Each day as we cope with these demands, we initiate our own changes. We grow and develop new knowledge, new skills or abilities. We go on a diet, upgrade our life-style, or assume a new financial obligation. We experiment with different perspectives and approaches.

Each change triggers a response, however slight, in our systems. Therefore we are constantly processing our responses to the thousands of stressors we experience each day. Much of the time we are unaware of either the stressor or our response because the body functions so automatically. However, if the stressor becomes constant or increased in intensity, our stress repsonse increases to an uncomfortable level.

Consider, for example, entering a dimly lit room and turning on a lamp. You may not be acutely aware of the adjustment your pupils make to the additional light. However, if you were in a very dark room and someone were to repeatedly turn off and on a bright light, your body's response would be increased, and you would probably begin to feel discomfort. Controlling your body's response would be as simple as closing your eyes, leaving the room, or requesting that the light be either turned off or left on.

Stress Can Be a Positive Factor

Some people function best when experiencing a fairly high level of stress. Amy cheerfully juggles a busy schedule which includes caring for four stepchildren, two children of her own, remodeling her house (while keeping it spotlessly clean), starting a consulting business, singing in the church choir, and working 40 hours a week for a school district. When any of her friends call, she is always ready to drop what she's doing and drive to the airport, run errands, baby-sit, or listen to a two-hour recital of personal woe. Amy admits that people often comment on her fantastic level of energy.

"But I have to be involved in a lot of things," she confides, "Otherwise, life would be so boring!"

A controlled number of stressors can have a positive effect on life, for most of us would be bored by life characterized by sameness. A few of the positive effects of stress are:

1. Personal motivation

Setting goals and striving to reach them motivates us to grow and achieve.

2. Increased productivity

Having goals which are just beyond an easy reach causes us to stretch our levels of output, and the payoff in inner satisfaction is quite invigorating.

3. A positive self-image

Developing and exercising one's talents and abilities build a positive self-concept.

4. Relaxation as a reward

Relaxing is most appreciated when "earned" by a stint of hard work.

5. Flexible attitudes

Successfully coping with routine changes develops one's skills for decision-making and problem solving, and helps one maintain a flexible attitude.

6. Breaks the monotony.

Living with a limited number of stressors keeps one from slipping into a rut from which escape is difficult.

The Dangers of Stress

Too many stressors can be dangerous to a person's

emotional and physical health. A person is experiencing stress overload when he is no longer maintaining the overall homeostasis (natural balance) of all physical systems functioning normally. Stress overload occurs at different levels for different people. What may be an excessive stress level for one person, may be easily handled by another who has developed the skills required for controlling the internal response.

The first step in learning to cope is to recognize what specific stressors we personally find most difficult to endure. Is it frustration—being kept from reaching our objective? Is it conflict—having to choose between opposing people or demands? Is it pressure—being forced to increase or intensify our activity?

Interestingly enough, the demand for intensified or increased activity need not be negative in order to create a stress overload. A bride and groom planning a Christmas wedding with a honeymoon in Europe, after which they are coming home to a beautiful, new home and a job promotion for one of them, would not feel that these "demands" were negative. But all these events exact a penalty in the form of internal stress.

Dr. Thomas Holmes and colleagues at the University of Washington School of Medicine developed a Social Readjustment Rating Scale which is widely used (especially in the military service) to determine susceptibility to disease.

The scale lists 43 life events and gives each a weighted point value. An accumulated point value of 150—199 in one year indicates a mild problem—a 37 percent chance of experiencing physical symptoms of stress overload. From 200 to 299 suggests a moderate problem with a 51 percent chance of experiencing a change in health. A score of over 300 is an indication of probable serious illness.

Figure 3-1
Social Readjustment Scale

Rank	Life Event	Mean Value
1	Death of spouse	100
2	Divorce	73
3	Marital separation	65
4	Jail term	63

5	Death of close family member	63
6	Personal injury or illness	53
7	Marriage	50
8	Fired at work	47
9	Marital reconciliation	45
10	Retirement	45
11	Change in health of family member	44
12	Pregnancy	40
13	Sex difficulties	39
14	Gain of new family member	39
15	Business readjustment	39
16	Change in financial state	38
17	Death of a close friend	37
18	Change to different line of work	36
19	Change in number of arguments with spouse	35
20	Mortgage over $10,000	31
21	Foreclosure of mortgage or loan	30
22	Change in responsibilities at work	29
23	Son or daughter leaving home	29
24	Trouble with in-laws	29
25	Outstanding personal achievement	28
26	Wife begin or stop work	26
27	Begin or end school	26
28	Change in living conditions	25
29	Revison of personal habits	24
30	Trouble with boss	23
31	Change in work hours or conditions	20
32	Change in residence	20
33	Change in schools	20
34	Change in recreation	19
35	Change in church activities	19
36	Change in social activities	18
37	Mortgage or loan less than $10,000	17
38	Change in sleeping habits	16
39	Change in number of family get-togethers	15
40	Change in eating habits	15
41	Vacation	13
42	Christmas	12
43	Minor violations of the law	11

In the case of the wedding couple, the cumulative score just for the month of December might include the following points:

Life Event	Point Value
Marriage	50
Gain of a new family member	39
Change in financial state	38
Mortgage of over $10,000	31
Change in responsibilities at work	29
Change in living conditions	25
Revision of personal habits	24
Change in residence	20
Change in sleeping habits	16
Change in eating habits	15
Vacation (honeymoon)	13
Christmas	12
Total	312

Those 312 points would then have to be added to any others accumulated in the preceeding 12 months to determine the stress level of the couple.

If this were a second marriage that included children from a previous marriage, the new stepparent would have to add 39 points for each stepchild (gain of a new family member) to the 312 points.

That means:

1 stepchild $= 312 + 39 = 351$
2 stepchildren $= 312 + 78 = 390$
3 stepchildren $= 312 + 117 = 429$
4 stepchildren $= 312 + 156 = 468$
5 stepchildren $= 312 + 195 = 507$

These high totals should serve as a caution to the couple to minimize or eliminate as many other life changes as possible.

As we develop an awareness of our own stress level, we can make better decisions about our abilities to take on additional pressures which might prove hazardous to our health.

Defining the Stress Response

The body's physical and chemical response to stressing conditions dates back to primitive days when one of the more important stressors was physical danger. Today's "dangers" are just as real, although usually more psychological than physical.

Whatever the source of the stress, the body responds in three stages, a process which Dr. Hans Selye in <u>Stress Without Distress</u> calls the "general adaptation syndrome" (GAS).

First, in the alarm stage, the body releases hormones and gears up for either fight or flight. Next, in the resistance stage, the body either adapts or resists the stressor. The energy drain during this stage is phenomenal. If the stressor continues, the third stage is exhaustion, when the energy is totally depleted. Carried to the extreme, with no intervention, exhaustion results in death. See Figure 3-2

One of the current theories about coping with stress is that we have a finite amount of energy at our disposal. A large proportion of this energy is required to maintain the body's physical systems, i.e., circulatory, muscular, endocrine, lymphatic, nervous, and digestive. The remaining energy is divided between physical, mental, and emotional activities. The body almost automatically distributes the energy appropriately and establishes its own homeostasis (natural balance) for normal routine.

Figure 3-2
General Adaptation Syndrome

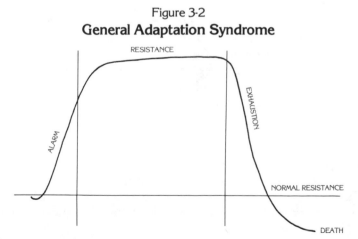

When the GAS is triggered, the balance is upset as energy is diverted from other areas to support the stress repsonse. If the stress is short-lived, the body quickly returns to homeostasis. If the stress is prolonged, sufficient energy to maintain a healthy body is no longer available and illness may occur. The physical symptoms will vary, depending upon an individual's inherited predisposition for disease. The more common illnesses or symptoms are: insomnia, heachaches, colds, flu, allergies, impotence, ulcers, colitis, asthma, dermatitis, hypertension, premature aging, bronchitis and emphysema, diabetes, heart disease, tuberculosis, and even cancer, according to recent research. See Figure 3-3.

We are all familiar with the stress response cycle. Sometimes we accept many crises with a smile, but at other times we can't take even one more demand without it becoming the proverbial last straw. Somewhere along the way we have used up our flexibility, our coping strength, and have begun to run on reserve energy as we head straight for exhaustion. Watch for the signs that you are using up your reserve.

—Little interruptions to the schedule or small demands become impossible obstacles. Their existence becomes a deliberate, personal attack. You **know** that the plumber didn't deliberately decide not to show up after you took the entire day off work just to wait for him. He probably had an emergency. But you **feel** that somehow you were singled out to be inconvenienced.

—Paradoxically, while little things seem to immobilize a person running on reserve energy, major problems seem almost insignificant and are often easily resolved.

—Excessive irritability, fatigue, change in sleeping habits, intestinal disturbances, weight change, respiration problems, heart irregularities, depression, general dissatisfaction, inability to make decisions, and apathy or a loss of creativity are other early warning signs of near exhaustion.

Perhaps one of the easiest ways to recognize that we are starting to operate in the danger zone is a persistent, nagging conviction that if too many more things go wrong, we won't be able to cope. Until we cross over into our reserve, the question of whether or not we can cope doesn't enter our minds. We feel capable and strong.

Figure 3-3
Etiology of Stress

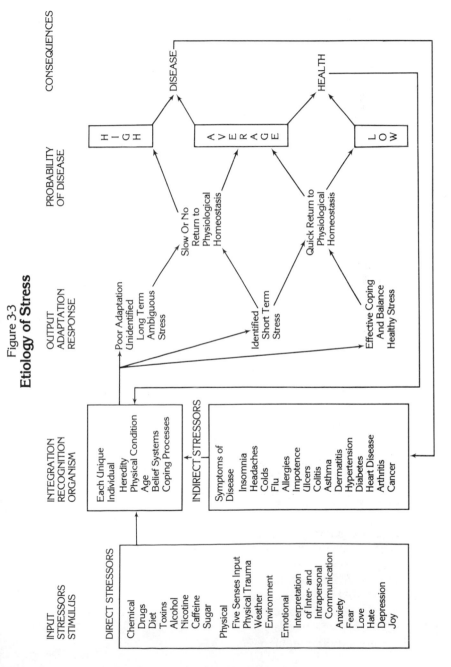

43

Unfortunately, we tend to live up to the very limits of our resources. We spend all of our incomes, so that we have to have insurance policies to cover emergencies. We schedule our time so full that we can't fit in unexpected delays or demands. And often we accept as many stressors as we can handle not only with our normal but also with our reserve energies. As a result, unexpected stressors find us unable to cope effectively because there is no extra energy.

Heeding these early warning signs and intervening early decrease the likelihood of serious illness. Let's identify in detail some of the stressors in an instant family acquired through remarriage.

Stressors in Steprelationships

Some of the stressors in steprelationships include:

1. Changes
   —New spouse
   —New children (or a new parent for our children)
   —New house (or a new spouse in our house)
   —New in-laws
   —New roles (few couples draw the role lines in exactly the same way)
   —New time schedules to accomodate the new situation
   —New eating habits
   —New friends
   —New activities
   —New pressures
   —New conflicts
   —New problems to resolve ("My girls never did the things your boys do!")

2. Conflicts
   —About any of the changes listed above
   —About values
   —About opinions
   —About expectations
   —About desires
   —About needs
   —About wants

—About life-styles
—About timing (do-it-now versus do-it-later)
—About child rearing
—About almost anything, given two or more people under stress overload!

3. Pressures
—To be calm and coping in spite of the situation
—To be mature in the face of childish demands
—To be everything we were as a person before remarriage
—To succeed
—To be "perfect"
—To be a model for the children
—To be a witness for the Lord
—To live up to the expectations of ourselves and others for us

4. Emotional Pressures

Inherent in the stepfamily are extreme emotional pressures, feelings which we want to ignore, because to acknowledge them acknowledges our humanity in its most unvarnished reality.

There may be guilt from any number of sources, about many things:
—over the failure of the previous marriage;
—about having left children with the former mate;
—about secret feelings of near-hate for the ex-spouse of the mate or resentment of the stepchildren.

There may be jealousy or envy of other families whose problems seem smaller than ours.

There may be anxiety over trying to make emotional, financial, and psychological ends meet.

There may be feelings of inadequacy and failure when "coping" is the last way to describe your behavior.

There may be anger and hostility threaded through the tenderness of your love for your mate when everything seems to be going against you.

You will find that there are some stressors that are unique to your own family because of the variables involved. Take time to list these and to discuss them with your mate.

Effective Stress Management

"After next Saturday, stress won't be a problem to me! I'm taking a class," Carl boasted.

It's not that easy, Carl.

Stress management skills take time to learn. As the stress overload developed over a period of several weeks, maybe even years, so controlling internal responses in the face of external demands is not accomplished overnight.

1. Keep a written record.

Write down everything that triggers your stress response during a one-week period. Note the response and the time it took to "calm down" again. Rate each stressor on a scale of 1—20 (with 20 being strongest). At the end of a week, add up the number of times your stress response was triggered by a stressor rated between 15 and 20. (If the number is unusually high, try to eliminate as many of these stressors as possible during the next week).

2. Set priorities

Prioritize the stressors in your life. Select one or two that you want to resolve first. Give yourself permission to ignore other demands while you concentrate on these stressors. For example, give up your usual home-cooked meals two or three nights a week in favor of eating at McDonald's or any easy-to-prepare sandwiches. This could give Mom or Dad almost two extra hours on those days to do other things. For a short, specified period, deal only with priority demands. Don't try to do everything all of the time.

3. Allow God's input into your priorities.

While He has promised strength for everything we do (Philippians 4:13), He also has a few other comments for us.

Setting aside 20—30 minutes a day to read from God's Word and carefully contemplating what He is saying to us serves as a spiritual girding up against the stressors in life. The promises are innumerable. Try these:

"But seek ye first the kingdom of God and His righteousness; and all these things shall be added unto you." Matthew 6:33

"Thou wilt keep him in perfect peace, whose mind is stayed on Thee." Isaiah 26:3

"He giveth power to the faint; and to them that have no

might He increaseth strength. Even the youths shall faint and be weary, and the young men shall utterly fail: But they that wait upon the LORD shall renew their strength; they shall mount up with wings as eagles; they shall run and not be weary; and they shall walk and not faint." Isaiah 40:29-31

What a glorious promise! To have renewed strength to cope with any stressor! He is faithful.

Talk to God.

As important as listening to God's input is, the communication is not to be all one-sided. Share with Him those hidden feelings you are afraid to voice aloud to anyone else. Tell Him your fears. He understands the pain of unjust criticism, of being forgotten, of needing love. Ask for wisdom and guidance in setting priorities in your life. With His help, you can be more than a conqueror (Romans 8:37).

4. Use specific interventions.

Consider ways to eliminate or reduce the effects of your top priority stressors. Ten specific interventions are given later in this chapter. Practice these techniques as appropriate. Don't expect miracles; progress one step at a time.

5. Set up a reward system.

Whenever an intervention successfully reverses the stress response, reward yourself. The reward must be something you value and desire. For example: a new book, a new outfit, a fishing trip, or a special meal. The reward should come from yourself, not from others, although a little praise from peers may also be reinforcing.

6. Follow rules for good health.

The general rules of coping with stress will sound very familiar, for they are the basic guidelines given us by our parents, teachers, physicians, and health books for living a healthy life. This is understandable in that not following these rules weakens our body's ability to respond to stress which then intensifies and results in illnesses. So, we all know the basic rules, but few of us ever connected them with our anxiety problems. For review, these guidelines are:

a. Maintain a balanced life.

Some people don't balance work with play. They find it difficult to quit working and get involved in some activity for the sole purpose of enjoyment. Very active people who feel guilty about sitting around occasionally and doing nothing may need to give themselves permission to learn to loaf just a little. The person who does not balance work and play, does not give his body time to relax from the tensions of his life. Likewise there must be a balance between roles: spouse, person, parent (for the adults), and child (for the children). Balance is also needed between mental, social, physical, and spiritual activity.

b. Get enough sleep and rest.

Most adults require about six or seven hours of sleep per night. A regular lack of sleep prevents the body from building up the required resistance to tensions and illnesses.

c. Talk out negative feelings.

Almost every article one reads about stress management extols the value of having a personal confidant. Expressing feelings verbally often precludes the need to express them physically through tension and anxiety.

d. Have regular physical checkups.

It is important to go to one's doctor for periodic checkups. Identification of physical problems early on makes correcting them much easier. Keeping oneself fit results in a zest for living and ensures that one is in a position to handle routine stressors.

e. Avoid self-medication.

We are a nation of self-medicated people. We take tranquilizers when we feel uptight, pep pills when we're dragging and sedatives when we can't sleep. And the people who do this are not the uniformed young people who are out looking for experimentation and thrills; they are adults, often career professionals. However, the highs and lows created by these self-medications can get a person hooked into a never-ending cycle. And, the "solution," which is only temporary, turns out to be a long-term enemy and stressor itself.

f. Maintain a healthful diet.

Review the facts of nutrition and the concepts of eating regular, well-balanced meals. Understand the roles of vitamins and minerals in keeping the body in shape to cope with unexpected tensions. Establish and follow a sensible eating plan. Avoid refined sugars and carbohydrates as much as possible, for these deplete the body of the specific vitamins which are needed for coping with stress.

g. Exercise.

There is little doubt that most people could do with more exercise in their lives. Exercise plays a role in maintaining muscle tone, keeping the body systems functioning smoothly and in developing the ability to control one's physical response to unexpected stress.

Obviously, none of these general rules are news to us. Yet when we understand their importance in controlling our stress responses, we gain a new desire and commitment to incorporate them into our life-styles.

Selecting Specific Interventions

Following the general principles of effective stress management helps us develop coping strength so that new stressors do not traumatize the body unnecessarily. From a position of strength, we can then select the specific intervention we need to minimize our responses to individual stressors. A few of the possible interventions are given below.

1. Take a break.

Putting a few minutes between the stressor and the action required of you allows your automatic stress response to proceed, but under control. We are all familiar with the take-a-break technique. We stop struggling with the tax returns to watch a half hour of television. We put away a sewing project after ripping out the same seam three times. But there are other applications of this principle.

Example: Don is at work, concentrating on the report he is writing when the phone rings. He answers it, and immediately he is confronted with an angry school principal who is demanding that something be done immediately or little Pete will be expelled from third grade—forever!

Instantly Don's stress response is triggered because the endocrine system "assumes" he is under "attack." If Don is comfortable dealing with angry school principals, the stress response will quickly abate, and his body will return to homeostasis within a couple of minutes.

On the other hand, if Don recognizes that he is getting very uptight, he may need to take a little break from the call. He makes an appropriate excuse and hangs up promising to call back in just a few minutes. After a few deep breaths, a glass of fruit juice, and a moment or two of relaxation, Don is ready to call the principal. During the interim his body has calmed down, responding to the lack of an "attack."

When Don initiates the call, he is in control of himself and of the situation. His body does not feel under attack, and even the hostility of the school principal will not be a significant stressor, since it was anticipated and not a surprise. Don gets the facts and negotiates an acceptable resolution to the problem.

The take-a-break technique is useful in situations in which you are unexpectedly confronted and feel unprepared for the battle.

However, avoidance is only effective as a coping technique when it is a temporary measure. You cannot successfully avoid a stressor for very long. Sooner or later you will have to resolve the problem.

2. Learn to relax.

Most people do not know how to relax. If asked what they do to relax, people usually respond that they play tennis, bowl, read, or have some other hobby. Yet these activities are recreation, not relaxation. Relaxation is turning off stimuli as much as possible so that both your mind and your body are at rest.

Just telling oneself to relax doesn't usually work. Relaxation of tensed muscles is a skill which requires practice. First, one relaxes each muscle group. Then one learns to relax several groups at the same time. Finally, one can relax the entire body at once.

Several different audio cassettes are available commercially which guide the learner through relaxation exercises until the skill is mastered. Many colleges, health centers, and private vendors offer classes in relaxation techniques that are very helpful in case you are one of those people who do not know how to relax.

A comparison of the physiological responses under stress conditions and in relaxation would look like this:

Physiological Response	Under Stress	In Relaxation
heart beat	increase	decrease
blood pressure	increase	decrease

respiratory rate	increase	decrease
oxygen consumption	increase	decrease
metabolism	increase	decrease
muscle tension	increase	decrease
blood flow to muscles and brain	increase	decrease
blood flow to G. I. tract and skin	decrease	increase
skin conductance level	increase	decrease
alpha brain waves (8-13 Hz)	decrease	increase

When developing the ability to relax, you must also develop an awareness of when to relax. Relax at the first symptoms of stress. (You do not wait to attempt total relaxation when you are all tensed up and twitching!) In this way the ability to relax becomes invaluable because it can be used in action, on the job, or at home.

3. Use biofeedback.

Through the use of biofeedback machines you can train yourself to control your stress response, to relax, and even to control internal systems once thought to be strictly autonomous.

4. Take a class.

If your lack of a specific skill or body of knowledge is a significant stressor in your life, take a class to correct the problem. Community colleges, universities, and adult education programs are only a few of the institutions that offer classes, seminars, workshops or mini-conferences on almost every possible topic you could wish for. Correcting a perceived skill deficiency will alleviate the pressure you are experiencing.

5. Limit the amount of work brought home from the office.

If you are in the habit of bringing work home every night, you are probably perpetuating the feelings of stress from the day, right into the evening and through the night. Even if you decide not to do the work once you get home, there are problems because the briefcase sits there in silent mockery all evening. Very stressful! Rules may include:

If you must bring work home, then don't bring everything. Select just one or two things that can be done within a reasonable amount of time, and then you will feel good about yourself for having completed what you intended to do.

Work in only one place in the home. It may be the study, the library, the kitchen, the den, or even the desk in the bedroom. Don't work just anywhere you happen to be sitting. Keep the work you do at home localized instead of "contaminating" the entire home with it.

Try delegation on the job. Perhaps others can't do the job as well as you can, but they can learn.

6. Engage in a highly reinforcing activity after coming home from work.

Many people who never carry a briefcase home, take the job home in their heads. They continue pondering the problems and issues still unsolved at the office. The best intervention for this stressor is to engage in a highly reinforcing activity for the first half hour you are home from work. This may be listening to the relaxation tapes or the stereo, watching television, reading the newspaper or a book, playing with the children, or working on a hobby. The activity must be reinforcing, pleasant, and different from work. So if you write on the job, don't go home and immediately start to work on the great American novel.

l7. Learn to make decisions and let them go.

No one makes perfect decisions all of the time. However, studies show that the most successful decision-makers are those who consider alternatives, make a selection, implement their decision, and then let that decision go. They do not continue to rethink the issue and wonder if they made the right decision. Most frequently there is not one right decision. Sometimes the alternatives are roughly equal. Therefore, any chocie is acceptable and practical as long as people are aware of the consequences of the decision and act accordingly.

The specific system of decision-making is not necessarily of great importance, for there are many ways to make informed decisions. What is important is that there be no redecision without new, external data.

8. Obtain closure.

A backlog of unresolved situations, projects, or issues can be a significant stressor. Obtaining closure relieves the pressure. Schedule one day to run the errands, write the letters, clean the closets, make minor repairs, or to do whatever is nagging at you from your mental back burner. Although you will be tired that night, you will experience not only immense satisfaction but also a surge of new energy because you have relieved the pressure.

9. Be assertive.

Being assertive means taking the responsibility for your own needs, feelings, ideas, and actions. It puts you back in control of yourself and your life. Assertive is the opposite of passive and the antithesis of aggressive. Acquiring assertive skills gives you the ability to be in charge of your stress response.

As each person acquires assertive skills, the entire family benefits. Take time to talk with your family about the stressors you are experiencing. Invite all family members to share their perspectives of the pressures you share and their individual responses to the situation. Seek to set priorities, and develop action plans as a family.

10. Experience acceptance and forgiveness.

The images of super-parent, wonder-person, and fantastic-child will have to go. Strive for OKness. That is reachable. Accepting your own limitations and those of others makes it possible to live with stress without distress.

Acceptance makes forgiveness possible, because acknowledging that people are not perfect admits that they will make mistakes.

Through forgiveness we experience healing of the wounds caused by our mistakes. Let us be forever willing to forgive others so that our relationships are not broken. Forgiveness from God is available for the asking (1 John 1:9). Although our family and friends may be somewhat reluctant to forgive our wrongs, they usually do when we prove our repentance through restitution. But we are not completely healed until we forgive ourselves. Some people seem to be unable to forgive any imperfections in their own lives. We must remember that a failure to forgive ties us to an unresolved past and prevents our personal and spiritual growth. If God, the most holy and righteous judge, forgives us in Christ, how can we refuse to do the same?

If you recognize that you are experiencing extreme stress overload to the point of being incapable of extricating yourself, you may want to seek professional assistance in selecting the specific interventions which will be the most help to you.

The End of Your Rope

I walked into an office last week, and the words on a poster caught my eye. "When you get to the end of your rope, tie a knot and hang on." By following the principles outlined in this chapter, you will have the strength to do just that! And more! For through effective stress management you learn to stop stress early on; and usually you avoid getting to the end of your rope in the first place.

For Further Reading

Herbert Benson, The Relaxation Response (New York: Morrow and Company, 1976)

Robert Collier Page, M.D., F.A.C.P., How to Lick Executive Stress (New York: Cornerstone Library, 1977)

Robert H. Schuller, Turn Your Stress into Strength (Irvine, CA: Harvest House Publishers, 1978)

Hans Selye, Stress Without Distress (New York: J. P. Lippincott, 1974)

Hans Selye, The Stress of Life (New York: McGraw-Hill, 1956)

Robert L. Wise, Your Churning Place (Glendale, CA: Regal Books, 1977)

Part Two
Demystifying
the Roles

Chapter Four
Stepmothers

⋙ ⋘

"Having a stepfather is OK," said 10-year-old Jay emphatically, "but a stepmother is yucky!"

This from a boy who has had two stepmothers and who has been very close and loving with both!

Stepmotherhood as a general concept has been much maligned. Fairy tales tell of "wicked" stepmothers. Shakespeare wrote of cruelty and dishonesty in steprelationships. And the classics show the various adversities that befall children who have the misfortune of having a stepmother! Since little has been done to force some reality into the general connotation of stepmotherhood, it is no wonder that the negative perception persists.

True, there are wicked, cruel, uncaring stepmothers, just as there are wicked, cruel, and unfeeling mothers. But both are in the minority when compared to the total population of women raising children.

In fact, sometimes a stepmother is in a better position than the natural mother to have a positive influence on the development of a child.

—If the stepmother is married to a noncustodial father, her contact is probably limited to short-term visits during which it is possible to maintain calm consistency. The custodial parent can be so bogged down with the day-to-day problems that survival becomes more critical than teaching the child.

—If the stepmother does not have a career outside of the home, she has more time to interact with children than does a mother who must work to support her family.

—Some people are better at parenting than others. A stepmother may be one of those people who have just the right blend of patience, wisdom, and humor to make parenting a joy.

—If children, especially adolescents, are resentfully struggling with their mother for independence, they sometimes turn to their stepmother for the nurturing they still desire and need.

Whether or not the relationship betwen the stepmother and the children works out depends on so many variables that neither success nor failure can be credited to the stepmother alone.

So Many Resentments

Most stepmothers find their first year mined with hidden resentments, and they seem to explode at the worst possible times. These unexpected hostilities are difficult to resolve before a major explosion because they are often repressed until the pressure becomes too much to control. Some are only nebulous feelings rather than identified, specific objections. Here are typical resentments—

1. From the ex-wife

New wives are often accused of having broken up the previous marriage, whether or not there is any basis in fact for the allegation. Protective of their "territorial rights," ex-wives may operate on a I-may-not-want-him-but-I-don't-want-anyone-else-to-have-him premise. Therefore, new wives are to be resented. Or perhaps the problem is envy of the new wife who is making a marriage work which the ex-wife couldn't All too often the basis of the hostility is the terrifying fear that the children will come to love the stepmother more than their own mother.

Sometimes the two women can get together and honestly talk over their roles and relationships to each other. Even without becoming close freinds, the women can allay one another's secret fears and often eliminate resentments. Such communication may be impossible or unprofitable. But as long as the new wife can maintain a healthy perspective toward the ex-wife, these resentments can be treated as minor problems rather than major disasters.

2. From her own children

A mother who remarries a man with children faces the possibility of resentment from her own children. Having to share a mother's love, time, and attention with a stepfather and stepsiblings is not always a pleasant prospect to children who may have had their mother to themselves for several years.

Recognizing ahead of time that her children may feel left out in the new relationship, a mother will want to take time to openly discuss fears and expectations with her children. A little understanding and a lot of reassurance that they are still loved as much as before will go a long way in helping children adjust to having a stepfather in the home.

3. From her husband

Fathers who have not resolved their guilt over the "failure" of their former marriage or who are overindulgent with their children tend to resent any conflicts between their children and their new wives. In these situations the new wives are expected to not only support but also to share in the fathers' attempts to "make it up to the children." Any comments about "spoiling the children" or about "overdoing things" may trigger a major marital battle.

A wife can sometimes help her husband see how he is using inappropriate actions to assuage guilt or failure feelings by inviting him to share with her those feelings. However, this conversation is most effective during a quiet, neutral sharing time rather than as part of an emotional conflict over a specific incident. Sometimes a wife cannot help her husband in this area, so she must commit him to the Lord's care and let the Holy Spirit work out the healing of old wounds.

4. From the stepchildren

Stepchildren perceive, or dream up, many excuses for resenting dad's new wife.

—Because she broke up their home (whether or not she did);

—Because she's keeping dad from remarrying mom (whether or not he ever would);

—Because she's too young (or old);

—Because she does things differently from mom (whether or not mom's way is desirable);

—Because she makes dad happy and is important to him;

—Because she shares dad's time, love, and attention;

—Because she can . . .

—Because she can't . . .

A resentful, hateful child is difficult to love, even when one understands some of the fears and insecurities behind the negativism. Building that bridge of communication often seems a one-sided effort from the adult to a nonresponsive child.

Children who are responsive to a prospective stepmother sometimes change suddenly when dad marries her. Before the marriage she is perceived as a special friend of theirs and dad's. She is fun to be with as they do special things together. When she tells them to do something or asks them not to do other things, she is obeyed because they want to please this special friend. Even though she is an adult, she is often viewed as an equal. Then she marries dad, and suddenly she is no longer an equal or a friend. She is a parent with full authority to give orders and withhold pleasures. This shift in roles may be experienced by the children as a betrayal of trust, to be deeply resented.

Because building the relationship with the stepchildren is such a unique and critical issue, several ideas are explored in chapters nine through twelve of this book.

5. From within

"I have a few resentments myself," Rhoda admits. "I try so hard to live up the expectations of my husband, stepchildren, and myself, but I get so tired. I have rights in this family, too!"

She's correct. She does have rights. Deep within that inner person even the best of us experience resentments when we feel that our wants or needs are not being met. Stepmothers are given many opportunities to feel left out, forgotten, and not valued in the same way as others:

—When part of her paycheck goes to support his ex-wife and children;

—When the ex-wife makes excessive demands on her husband and he meets them;

—When the children (his, hers, or theirs) intrude;

—When she is continually compared unfavorably to the ex-wife;

—When there is never enough time to meet all of the demands;

—When her husband fails to support her in front of his children;

—When she is expected to assume total responsibility for his children while he abdicates his share.

Unresolved resentments, like termites in a house, eat away at the relationship weakening its structure. These resentments bring bitterness and anger and alienate people one from the other. Thus, as resentments are recognized and owned, they must be openly confronted in an attempt to free the relationships from these destructive forces. Each family member's needs and desires must be given considered attention. In an atmosphere of loving acceptance, fears can be allayed, constructive criticism can be accepted, and hurts healed through forgiveness. Paul urges this course of action in Ephesians 4:31-32: "Let all bitterness and wrath and anger and clamor and evil speaking be put away from you, with all malice. And be ye kind one to another, tenderhearted, forgiving one another, even as God for Christ's sake hath forgiven you."

A wise stepmother will recognize that at times she is going to be caught in the middle of situations she didn't anticipate. As a result her responses may be overwhelmingly negative. But in marrying into a stepfamily, she has taken a vow before God to give of herself to this new relationship. She will need to be able to:

—openly discuss her feelings with her husband;
—ensure that her relationship with the Lord is kept open and strong; and
—be willing to try alternate approaches to resolve problems.

Reaping Rewards

"Wally is well behaved, obedient, happy, and doesn't use baby talk anymore," boasts Fay with pardonable pride.

Six-year-old Wally had come to live with her just a couple of months after her marriage to his dad. As the baby of the family Wally had never been required to abide by the standards of behavior expected of his older brothers, and therefore he was never disciplined. Through long hours of loving instruction and patient reinforcement of positive actions, Fay had helped Wally prepare for the realities of first grade. She had disproved his kindergarten teacher's assertion that Wally had a serious learning disability. "The only reason that Wally didn't know colors or the alphabet and didn't have a large vocabulary was that no one had taken time to teach him," Fay explained. When Wally excelled in school, Fay felt rewarded for her efforts.

The rewards of being a stepparent are the same as those of

being a parent. We are rewarded (often belatedly) when our children appreciate us, respect us, love us, or imitate us. We are rewarded when our children succeed in their lives because of our investment in their development. The difference between parenthood and stepparenthood lies in the fact that in the latter case one is investing in the lives of someone else's children.

No matter how wonderful the stepmother is, she never takes the place of the biological mother. This fact may hurt the stepmother who feels she has been far more of a "mother" than the natural mother ever was. But one must keep in mind that the tie between child and parent goes beyond the surface interactions between them. That people want to identify with their natural parents is evident by the fact that many adults who were adopted children expend much time and money searching out their biological parents

However, just because a stepparent cannot take the place of a natural parent does not mean that the steprelationship cannot be loving, strong, and fulfilling.

Healthy Relationships

Keeping the relationships healthy challenges a stepparent's resourcefulness at times; and juggling priorities, mediating conflicts, and keeping the homelife operational significantly drains one's energy. Still, each individual relationship must be carefully nurtured if the family unit is to be strong.

In the following discussion of relationships that the stepmother must attend to, many of the principles also apply to stepfathers.

1. With self

When Jill remarried, she kept on with her graduate studies and her teaching job. She felt it was important to continue to fulfill her intellectual needs.

Assuming responsibility for personal needs is appropriate behavior, as long as this does not violate another's rights. A sense of personal worth enables interaction with others in a positive way. Several people who were interviewed offered ideas for taking care of self.

—Diane keeps a studio where she can paint in the solitude she requires.

—Marge joined a health spa and works out a couple of evenings a week.

—Irene belongs to a reading discussion club that meets one evening a week.

—Elizabeth is a guest lecturer, which sometimes takes her out of town for a couple of days.

Whatever it takes to reinforce the inner self without damaging the family relationship is worth the investment. For a person who is not whole, and needs to reinforce the inner self, it may be a matter of looking to others to fill in the gaps. People with no self-confidence want others to be confident for them. Shy people depend on others to draw them into conversation and activities. People with poor self-images need others to reinforce their worth. Expecting someone else to take the responsibility for personal deficiencies sets up a dependency in the relationship which is an unfair burden to the partner. Those who take responsibility for their own growth and personal development can relate to their partners as whole people.

2. With the Lord

A man tried to explain his problem to a psychiatrist.

"My wife and I live in a $200,000 house, drive new Cadillacs, entertain lavishly, both at home and on our yacht, travel all around the world . . ." he paused to breathe.

"That's quite a life-style," the psychiatrist commented thoughtfully. "What's wrong with it?"

"There's no problem with our life-style," the man replied. "My problem is that I only earn $150 a week!"

How ridiculous! To try to live a $1,500-a-week life on a $150-a-week income! And yet, people often do—overcommitting themselves by trying to live superhuman lives with only natural strength, and consequently failing. God's strength is needed to live the victorious life as new creatures in Christ. In Ephesians 6, Paul urges putting on the whole armor of God in order to withstand attack. In John 15, Christ asserts that without Him, people can do nothing. Truly, successful human relationships are only possible when people are right with God.

Communicating with God on a regular basis provides insights that are helpful in resolving the problems of everyday life. Personal assurance of God's love is revealed. And the success promised in Psalm 1:1-3 is experienced.

3. With the mate

"I never dreamed there was anyone like Tim" Sara sighed happily. Eagerly she adopted her new husband's habits, ideas, preferences, and hobbies. If ever her desires conflicted with his, she gave in without a murmur. She seemed to live for Tim.

Nine years later they were divorced.

Within a few months Sara remarried. Still bitter over Tim's rejection "after all she had given him," Sara promised herself she would never be the "giver" again. And so she staunchly held her ground on even the smallest disagreement. She never initiated reconciliations. True to her promise, she did not give of herself to her new husband.

They were divorced within two years.

If any marriage is to work, both partners must be willing to love one another freely and be sincerely committed to submitting one to the other. This mutual commitment must not be overlooked in the hectic family schedule.

Research studies show that the husband-wife relationship has a profound effect on the children. "Children act out the marriage," says counselor Tom Russell. "If the relationship is good, the children tend to be well adjusted. If the relationship is faulty, children tend to exhibit behavior problems."

Successful couples have made sure they took the time to be romantic and affectionate with each other. They enjoyed being alone together. Because thoughtfulness and courtesy go a long way in a marriage, they remember birthdays, anniversaries, special interests, or preferred foods.

4. With the children

There are three types of stepmothers:

a. those who do not have children of their own; b. those who have children of their own, living with them; and c. those whose children live elsewhere (i. e., with their father, or in their own homes). Previous experiences with developing successful parent-child relationships will influence the way a stepparent interacts with the stepchildren.

Learning to live with other people's children is indeed a challenge. Nancy often fought the urge to leave during the first two years of her remarriage. For seven years she had lived alone with her sons (who were 11 and 15 by the time she remarried Marvin). A regular family schedule had evolved which suited all three. The boys, like most children, understood mom well enough to know when to leave her alone and when to ask for special favors. Then homelife was fairly free from conflicting needs or wants.

Marvin's children, all four of whom were under ten years of age, were totally unfamiliar with house rules, schedules, or the signs of a mother who is at the end of her strength. When Marvin took a second job to relieve the financial strain, Nancy's determination to overcome all obstacles in her new marriage was put to the test. Four years passed before Nancy felt able to relax somewhat. The marriage and the family relationships survived.

Although each family situation is unique, young stepmothers whose stepchildren are under 10 years old do tend to develop close relationships. On the other hand, blended families where both mates have adolescents are the least successful for the obvious reasons. The greatest period of stress for a biological family is the children's adolescence. Combining two adults and one or more adolescents from two different families to form a new family is to attempt stepkinship under the most adverse conditions possible.

Stepparents with children of their own may find it difficult to be impartial. Regardless of their feelings (for some people are more lovable than others), stepparents should be careful to keep their "courtroom decisions" as fair and equal as possible. And yet, it is imperative that they take time out to be alone with their own children who must not suffer a loss of intimacy just because others have joined the family group.

Weekend stepparents face a double challenge—to develop two life-styles that are expected to interface smoothly. For most of the time the noncustodial couple's homelife routine is adult centered. Then, at least twice a month the children arrive for the weekend, and the alternate life-style begins.

At least part of the weekend, the children usually want to be alone with their parent, which excludes the stepparent. Sometimes this is resented. "Since we both work all week, I look forward to my weekends with Roger. I don't want him to take off with his kids without me!" one young stepmother shared. But other women view these "alone times" as opportunities to do the things they've been wanting to do.

—Velma has lunch with a single woman friend.

—Wanda goes to a romantic movie (her husband hates them).

—Trisha curls up in front of the fire with a good book.

—Kim does her housecleaning with no one under foot.

—Phyllis goes window shopping.

Designing the relationship that will work between step-parent and stepchild is a very individual undertaking, for people are so different that what works for one person doesn't always work for another.

5. With the ex-spouses

Ex-spouses have a way of intruding into new marriages, partly because they are still co-parents of children who share both homes. A second reason is that the years spent together cannot be erased. Emotional ties (both loving and antagonistic) are difficult to completely sever. Also, unresolved issues from former marriages have a tendency to carry over into new marriages. Consequently the relationship with both of the ex-spouses requires consideration.

Ideally a cooperative arrangement can be developed for sharing the children and making decisions related to their welfare, while maintaining a hands-off attitude toward the other aspects of each other's lives. However, the very reasons why a couple got divorced (differing values, priorities, life-styles and ideas) often preclude the totally cooperative approach.

6. With a friend

Everyone needs a best friend of the same sex, someone who will listen without judging or proffering instant solutions to the major perplexities. That person is one who keeps confidences, in short is an empathizing, accepting, loving confidant.

A best friend is needed when the inner well of strength has run dry or when affirmation from someone outside the marriage is needed. There come times when a person isn't ready to talk things over with the spouse yet because the anger is too intense or the pain is too deep. Talking over feelings with this friend first helps clarify the thoughts and sort out the feelings. Ranting, raving, yelling, or weeping is safe because there will be no repercussions. As the feelings are expressed and brought under control, personal strength is renewed and the problems are kept in perspective. Return to the family and problem resolution is then possible.

A Promise for Stepmothers

On those difficult days, stepmothers may want to consider the following paraphrase of Luke 6:27-38:

Love all those who seem to be your enemies, and do good to those that hate you. Bless those who resent you, and pray for those who are angry and hateful toward you. When your husband's ex-wife or children take that which is rightfully yours, give it freely without demanding equal compensation. Treat each member of your family the way you would like them to treat you. Loving your husband is easy, because he loves you in return. Anyone can love those who are loving. But if you will love and be kind to those who are unloving and hurtful, your reward will be great. If you are not judgmental and condemning, you will not be judged or condemned. Forgive and you will be forgiven. If you will give freely, you shall receive good measure—pressed down, shaken together, and running over. For what and how you give, you shall receive in kind.

Chapter Five
Stepfathers

Dinner had been a gourmet's delight in an elegant restaurant. In muted tones, the orchestra provided the romantic mood. The lights in the couple's eyes were more than a reflection of the candle flames. They were in love, and Larry had just proposed marriage.

As much as she loved Larry, Sandy was hesitant to verbalize the Yes in her heart. In the two years that she and Larry had been dating, he had yet to build a strong relationship with her three young sons. On occasion she had heard him make remarks which strongly implied that children were not part of his planned life-style. How then could he propose? Had he considered all of the ramifications of marrying the mother of three boys?

Sandy voiced these questions gently, not wanting to dampen the ardor of the moment, or to seem unromantic.

"The kids are no problem, Honey." Larry assured her. "I love you enough to accept the fact that you have kids. They're just part of the package!"

Although not completely reassured, Sandy accepted the proposal. The engagement lasted two months during which Larry made a conscious effort to incorporate Sandy's boys into his life. "I'm too self-centered to enjoy taking the responsibility for nurturing, instructing, and developing children. I don't want to lose you, but if we go through with our wedding plans, we are all going to be hurt later on. So I guess this is good-bye," he told Sandy one night.

A painful, but wise decision.

A Package Deal
Stepchildren are more than just "part of the package" that

comes with a new spouse. They are people, new, individual members of the intimate family.

However, the fact that there are stepchildren is more often than not a given in second marriages. And, because our country's judicial system has traditionally given physical custody of minor children to the mother in divorce or dissolution cases, stepfathers can usually expect that their stepchildren will be in residence.

Living with someone else's children may be a difficult adjustment for a new husband for several reasons:

1. If he has never had children and has been living alone, how can he anticipate the new situation accurately?

He probably expects the house to be as neat in the evening as when he left in the morning. He may expect special snacks to still be in the kitchen cupboards when he wants them—five days after they were purchased. He may not understand about the "mysterious, unknown stranger" who causes all of the household damages when parents aren't around. And he, reasonably, may want to be alone with his wife more than seems possible with children in the house.

"It's not exactly the children themselves I resent. It's their constant presence. I mean, they're always there. Even when we're sitting alone after they are in bed asleep, we're not alone. Am I making any sense?" Harold asks.

Of course you are, Harold. Adjusting to living with another person is a process of dovetailing needs, wants, and priorities through continued interaction, until the motion becomes smoothly operational, much like two cog wheels in a mechanical apparatus. Because the friction of metal against metal could cause mechanical failure, cog wheels are kept well lubricated for as long as they are in motion. Just so relationships must be kept well protected with love to minimize the possibility of friction resulting in a family disaster. When the other person one is living with is a new spouse, the process is facilitated by the ecstacy of romantic love, something that is not a factor in the relationship with new stepchildren.

Easing into living in a family unit after living alone is facilitated when expectations are discussed with all members ahead of time. The man should feel free enough to explain that there are some considerations he really needs to cope effectively. These may include getting to read the paper first, shower first, or even having 20 minutes of quiet, uninterrupted alone time immediately upon returning home. Such seemingly small considerations cost other family members very little effort, but they can go a long way toward making a new stepfamily work.

2. If a man's own children live with the ex-spouse, his stepchildren may serve as constant reminders of his loss and trigger any number of inner responses.

Earl feels remorse that he never developed a close bond with his own children before his divorce.

Isaac tries too hard to have a perfect relationship with his stepchildren, who are substitutes for the sons he never sees. (They live 2,000 miles away, and the mother refuses him any contact, even though the court order reads "reasonable visitation.")

Fred tends to hold back a little from his three-year-old stepdaughter. The pain of losing his close relationship with his own daughter is too recent to allow him the freedom to risk another loss.

Sam finds that he must constantly remind himself that his style of communicating with children is unfamiliar to his stepchildren. His own children had learned to understand him well—but it had taken years to achieve!

Vince recognizes that his own children have suffered the loss of him as part of their daily homelife. So when they come to visit, he makes a special effort to reassure them of his continued love and support. He goes out of his way to listen to and share with them.

This common attempt to squeeze a couple of weeks' worth (or even more) of attention into a two-day weekend is sometimes resented by stepchildren. They consider it unfair.

Once again the solution to these different situations is for the family members to be understanding of the problem for the man involved. NOT trying to understand exactly how he feels and why he does what he does may imply disagreement with his reasoning and a judgment that he is behaving inappropriately. So, instead, try to be understanding and accepting, allowing him to work through his conflicting feelings, finding the behaviors with which he can accept his new relationships.

On the other hand, family members do have a responsibility to provide feedback to the man on their responses to his behaviors. Saying "You shouldn't do . . ." is judgmental. Saying "When you do thus and so, I feel . . ." is providing valuable feedback that helps a man decide on the behaviors he chooses to adopt.

3. If a man's children live with him and his new family, he may feel his relationships with the two sets of children being constantly compared by all members of the group.

It is unrealistic to expect that the relationships will be completely the same. A father has a history of relating to his own offspring. Between them, they have developed a workable system. On the other hand, his stepchildren have their own well-developed system of interacting with a parent. The two systems are probably different. Therefore, while the man may continue relating to his own children according to their system, the system which becomes operational with the stepchildren tends to be a compromise between the two systems—his and theirs.

The adjustment to living with other people's children is one which most stepfathers make successfully. In fact, one study revealed that a greater percent age of stepfathers had excellent relationships with their stepchildren than did stepmothers. Some sociologists explain that because men usually have careers outside of the home, their opportunities for interacting with stepchildren are limited, and therefore conflicts are minimized. However this argument seems somewhat invalid in a society where working wives are the norm.

Crime and Punishment

Even when the prenuptial discussions include child rearing and discipline, a couple will often find that they sometimes disagree on the proper way to respond to less-than-ideal behavior.

In steprelationships, natural parents usually give permission to their mates to discipline the children. However, that permission is often conditional as it is mentally qualified with "as long as I agree with the way you discipline at the time." Children are quick to sense division between their parents and to press their advantage with the more lenient adult in any given situation. Agreeing as a couple and family on standards of behavior and appropriate consequences for failure to meet those standards is one way to minimize discipline conflicts.

Discipline is the key word. A family is not a judicial system charged with meting out punishments for crimes. A family serves as an instructional institution for teaching children to be functional adults. The Scriptures give repeated admonitions for parents to train their children in the ways of the Lord. The learning process involves trying new behaviors and checking the outcomes to see if the desired goals were accomplished. Thus, training children and adolescents to assume the responsibility for their own behavior by accepting the natural consequences of the behavior is the key to effective disciplining. The ineffectiveness of punishment and the principle of natural consequences is clearly defined and illustrated in Dave and Jan Stoop's The Total(ed) Parent (Irvine, CA: Harvest House Publishers, 1978).

The Farmer Takes a Wife

Why do men marry?

To find companionship. To have their housekeeping needs met. To take care of a woman. To rescue children from being raised in a one-parent home. To have children. To replace a family lost through death or divorce. To be fulfilled. To be special to significant others who will love and care for them. To . . .

Many are the reasons for marriage. But perhaps the basic one is God's own observation that it is not good for a man to be alone. We have all discovered that life seems to have more meaning, and pleasures bring more joy when shared with a special friend. A spouse is intended to be that special friend.

"Sometimes I feel as if our friendship ended when we got married," George comments. "Before we were married, Ann and I used to collaborate on writing projects. She would get a sitter for her children and come over to my apartment. We each had our own desks and supplies. The quiet intimacy of creating together would be broken by heated discussion as we would struggle to help each other communicate complex concepts in a clear writing style. We always had a pot of coffee brewing—we drank gallons! Sometimes we would take a break and just sit in front of the fire and share. Hours would fly by unnoticed. It was a wonderful time.

"Then we got married. We set up a writing space in the family room. That didn't work because when we wanted to write, the kids wanted to watch TV. We tried writing at night after the children were asleep, but we were too tired to be creative. Right now we're set up in the corner of our bedroom, but we are often interrupted. Besides it's pretty crowded in there with all of our bedroom furniture as well as our writing supplies. I really miss those writing sessions."

As difficult as it may sometimes be to find ways to be alone together, the couple must strive to do so. (See Chapter 10.) For the strength of the family lies in the unity of the couple.

The Farmer Leaves a Wife

A man's relationship to his ex-wife affects his relationship with his new wife.

Any hostility between a man and his ex-spouse over support payments, custody, or visitation usually includes his new wife.

Sometimes the relationship with the ex seems "too good," Lori shares. "Paul was always running back to his ex-wife's house to repair the plumbing, trim the trees, or repair the car. I couldn't help myself. I began to feel jealous!"

Counselor Richard Baker explains this common situation. An ex-wife may continue to make demands on her husband after their divorce. As long as she hasn't found someone else to depend on, she may want to make him pay for having left her, or she may feel he owes her his continued assistance. The demands may be for household repairs, extra money, a change in the visitation plans, or any number of other things. The ex-wife (or ex-husband) learned how to manipulate her husband during their marriage, through such devices as threats, acting helpless, appealing to his love of the children. She knows how to get him to do what she wants.

So she calls, and he goes. Result:

The ex-wife is rewarded for her manipulation and will probably continue to make demands.

The new wife receives mixed messages. Her husband says he loves her and is happy with their game-free relationship. And yet, he continues to respond to the ex-wife's obvious game-playing. The ex-wife gets away with things the husband would never tolerate in the new wife. The man's actions seem to belie his words. Which is to be believed? Sometimes the new wife comes to wonder if her husband will leave her for his ex-wife, since he continues to return to her on demand.

The husband believes the situation to be perfectly clear. He continues to relate to his ex-wife as he did during their marriage because those were the ground rules of their relationship. He "can't" change the rules unilaterally. "She couldn't handle it." Or, "It's less disruptive to just do what she asks and get it over with" are typical explanations. And, contrary to his new wife's fears, the husband is not usually tempted to return to his former wife.

Roy comments, "I love my wife. We have the kind of open and honest relationship I've always wanted, but have never had before. Anytime I have to go over to my ex-wife's for one of her little jobs, I thank God for giving me my new wife."

Roy (and other husbands in similar situations) needs to delineate his responsibilities. Continued financial responsibility for spousal and child support, and ongoing responsibility for parenting his child, is not responsibility for taking care of the ex-wife's other needs. He is free from his commitment to cherish, protect, and care for her. His new commitment is to his new wife and to their new life together.

Follow the Leader

As the head of the house, the husband is charged with setting the spiritual pace for the family. A close relationship with God provides the strength to be a good role model and the wisdom to make good decisions.

In some respects, if he is to have a significant influence on the children, a stepfather is required to be a better leader than a natural father. Children tend to forgive natural parents for failing to be everything they should be. But stepparents don't always get that same level of acceptance. However, in both cases, the actions speak more clearly than the words. And so, a goal of stepfathers (and fathers) would be to say with Paul, "Follow me, even as I am a follower of Christ."

Chapter Six
Stepchildren

Children
The challenge
The beloved intruders
Those who put the "step" into a remarriage

The way children respond to the remarriage of one of their natural parents (and the subsequent gain of a new stepparent) depends on the perceived impact of the marriage on their own lives. If the anticipated impact is positive, then the response is positive. But if the impact seems threatening or disruptive, the response will be somewhat negative.

Conflicting Feelings

When a biological family is divided by a divorce, all members experience the loss. Gone is the intimate security of the family, never to be completely regained. The loss must be mourned as part of the healing process.

One of the first responses to a loss is to deny reality. The children in a divorce situation are almost always convinced that they were somehow responsible. Therefore, they conclude that if they were powerful enough to break up the family, then they are also powerful enough to reunite it again. And most children try to do just that—against all odds. When their efforts are unsuccessful, they experience guilt, frustration, anxiety, and other negative feelings.

A second mourning emotion is anger. Often children have a deep-seated anger toward the noncustodial parent for having "deserted" them. But because anger toward one's own parent is not always easy to accept in oneself, children frequently transfer this anger to the stepparent.

Sometimes children express their sense of loss through

sudden behavior changes: weeping, tantrums, a decline in scholastic achievement, antisocial mannerisms, or quiet withdrawal.

As the mourning experience is completed, the children find the wounds of loss are in the process of being healed. Because healing is an individual process, the mourning period varies in length from child to child. With healing comes the ability to form a modified relationship with the custodial parent, and also the noncustodial parent when contact is maintained.

Then one day the children are told that one of their parents is going to remarry. Immediately comes the recognition that the family life is about to change again. Instant fear! Will the change mean a loss of the child's importance to the parent?

I'm Scared!

Expecting to become less important to the parent after a remarriage, the child tries to regain the parents' attention. A child's resistance to the new marriage sometimes take the form of a one-person war against the couple. The cries for reassurance of personal importance can be very annoying to say the least.

—Jamie gets a fever (slight, but real) every time mom goes out with her husband-to-be.

—Tom quizes his mom's dates to determine their intentions of marrying his mother.

—Jeff said to the woman his father loves, "My mom is very successful. She says Dad can't take a woman who's successful and beautiful, because he feels it intimidates him. I guess that's why he dates you."

—Tim is openly rude.

—Patty committed a misdemeanor and wound up in Juvenile Hall.

Extremely hostile behaviors toward the (future) stepparent are indicative of a need for professional assistance to overcome irrational fears. Some of the fears which may be terrifying to children are:

1. Fear of disloyalty

Loving a stepparent may seem an act of disloyalty to the natural parent of the same sex, a concept which may be supported by an insecure parent.

76

Children experiencing this fear need to be reassured that the stepparent is not a replacement but an additional parent. Loving one does not preclude loving the other.

2. Fear of losing again

When children lose a parent through death or when one parent completely disappears after a divorce, children may become afraid to risk loving for fear of losing again. If their own parent deserted them, they reason, might not the stepparent?

As children learn to trust the stepparent, their fears should subside and allow them to reach out in love.

3. Fear of losing the parents' love

"Now that Mom (or Dad) has a new spouse, some of the time which used to be mine is now theirs. Is some of the love which was mine, now being channeled to the new spouse?" a child wonders.

A sensitive couple will ensure that the child has the attention needed from the biological parent to reaffirm the love between them.

Power, Power, Who's Got the Power?

Children, especially adolescents, are super at power plays. The favorite game of pitting one parent against the other is infinitely more challenging as children have the opportunity of playing one home (and set of parents) against the other home (and set of parents). Add in four sets of grandparents, and you can have a very destructive human chess game.

Parents who buy into the games find that children are more then willing to spy on, tattle, gossip, and tell stories about one home to the other. But children need to learn that each of their families has the right to privacy. Each home has a set of behavior standards and consequences for inappropriate behaviors. Neither home is 100 percent right nor 100 percent wrong; the homes are simply different models.

Another power ploy is testing the limits of acceptable behavior. With so many changes in the life-style because of a remarriage, children often attempt to renegotiate all of the standards of behavior from their single-parent home.

—"Do I still have to eat my carrots?"

—"Do I still have to go to bed at 9:30 p.m.?"

As difficult as the testing attempts may be, parents must

not give up and remove the limits, because children need limits. They fight rules, but even as they attack, they depend on the security of knowing where the limits are. Consistency of standards and discipline has proven most significant in parenting well-adjusted children.

I Need You!

Besides their basic food, clothing, and shelter needs, children have other needs.

A physical space of their very own is very important to children. The dimensions of the space will vary from family to family depending on available resources. Ideally, children would have a room of their own in each home. But if this is impractical, then a designated space will work: a bed, a corner, a drawer, or a closet. Having a specific, personal space gives a sense of belongingness to the child.

Spatial needs also include room to grow intellectually and emotionally. A child has the right to individual ideas, opinions, values and preferences which may not be consistent with those of the parent. Giving children intellectual and emotional space includes encouraging disclosure and discussion without condemnation.

2. Affirmation

Educator Ed Reed discusses the importance of parental affirmation and gives ideas for its use in the home.

To affirm someone communicates individual value and acceptance as a person—imperfections and all. To affirm builds positive relationships. To affirm reinforces a person's sense of self-worth. Affirmation feels good! Both to the receiver and the giver.

Parents have a responsibility before God to affirm their children. To show by actions that they are valuable and important as individuals. Only then can positive relationships develop, based on mutual trust, concern, and love. Only in an affirming home atmosphere can children open up and share their deepest thoughts, concerns, fears, and feelings. Then, lasting spiritual growth can occur.

Children remember the times a parent gives affirmation—and the times they don't!

One way to use affirmation is to assist a child in setting

goals, then affirming any progress which is made. Specific behaviors that parents may decide to affirm might include: sharing, obeying, praying, studying God's Word, winning a spiritual battle, kindness, loving sweetness, doing extra chores, taking a bath without being told to, or even just getting through the evening without a brother-sister quarrel!

Jesus affirmed people in His life for a variety of behaviors. He affirmed Mary of Bethany as she worshiped at His feet. He affirmed the widow who cast her mite into the temple treasury. He affirmed the faith of the centurion whose servant was healed. He affirmed His disciple Zacchaeus and the woman at the well by spending time with them.

Effective opportunities for affirming children include:

—Affirming the value of their ideas and encouraging creative thinking through listening attentively.

—Affirming their right to enjoyment by letting them share in the planning of family leisure time.

—Affirming their friendship by doing things together such as projects, working, playing, and talking.

—Affirming growing experiences by allowing risk taking without recriminations over resultant failures.

—Affirming their humanity by being fully human parents. (Free to be wrong sometimes. Unafraid to apologize).

—Affirming positive character traits by concentrating on one characteristic as a family for several weeks. (For example, if the trait is kindness, each family member would look for opportunities to be kind each day. During the dinner hour, individuals share their experiences and celebrate one another's acts of kindness).

—Affirming love by frequent hugging and touching one another.

3. Spiritual guidance.

As children grow up, they need to be guided into spiritual development. A guide is a person who knows the path because of having walked it before. A guide leads those who follow. Parents who worship with their families in church, who let the children observe their searching God's Word for answers and comfort, and who share their prayer life with the children are effective guides.

Children in stepfamilies are confronted with some hard-to-accept realities. They have suffered a loss of their natural family unit. Their identity is shaken. Stepparents have entered the picture. Their lives have been disrupted several times in different ways. Someone is to blame. Only through forgiveness comes the healing. And parents need to teach forgiveness by modeling an understanding spirit and a loving heart, ready to forgive.

4. Special help

Some children are unable to work through the fears, the hostilities, and the insecurities on their own. Sometimes more than parental love and guidance is required. Children who are having difficulty coping with the pressures in their world may become extremely possessive of their natural parent, resenting any attention given to someone else—especially the new stepparent. Or children may fantasize with great exaggeration about the noncustodial (or dead) parent or the family life prior to the divorce (or death of a parent). Hyperactivity, extreme nervousness, ultrasensitivity, and aggression are other signs of a need for special help. Whenever one family member needs professional help, the whole family is involved. The problem is not the individual's, it belongs to the family. When a lack of money prevents a family from seeing a counselor, they may find other community resources available.

—School districts often have family counseling services, or a psychologist on staff who may be consulted. Since children who act out at home often also act out at school, counseling services through the school may be appropriate.

—Many pastors have found key spiritual leaders in the church who also have professional counseling backgrounds, and are willing to be of assistance to members of the body who are in need.

—Local state, county, or city social service agencies provide crisis intervention services to families in need.

—Self-help groups such as those formed by the Stepfamily Foundation are becoming increasingly available in many of our cities.

Seeking professional assistance when needed is the wisest move a parent can make to help children living in step-relationships.

Who's Who?

Most children call their stepparents by their first names. In other families children select a nickname or an affectionate term of address. In some a form of mother or father is encouraged. Forcing children to identify the stepparent as mom or dad is not recommended; however, some children do so spontaneously and naturally. The important thing to remember is that stepparents' authority does not depend on what they are called.

Introductions are best kept simple. There is no need to emphasize the steprelationship by saying, "This is my stepson." Rather, "This is our son, Will." Insisting on specifying that a relationship is a "step" may give children the impression that the stepparent does not consider them as a real part of the family.

The Grass Is Always Greener

Fantasizing about a better life than the present one is a common human habit. Wanting to go live with the other parent is common among children whose time with their noncustodial parents is limited. That other home takes on all of the lure of Fantasy Island. Life there would certainly be far superior to what they have now!

Rarely are these fantasies diminished by parental reminders of realities. Neither should a parent belittle the other, for in tearing down the image of a parent, the child's self-image is also damaged. Most fantasies disappear as the children grow up, but sometimes they must be allowed to experience their dreams, because their obsession with it has caused them to develop antisocial behaviors to express their frustration with thwarted desires.

Jesus Was a Stepchild

Every boy or girl who experiences the emotional turmoil inherent in steprelationships has an understanding Lord. Jesus was a stepchild. He knew the feelings of having an earthly father question Him as He went about His Father's work in the temple. He knows today the kinds of problems a family encounters when all of the children do not share the same set of parents. He understands and cares.

Chapter Seven
The Parent Without Custody

Bitterness, anger, and guilt surround the issue of custody. Several people shared their experiences and feelings.

"At first I spent several evenings a week with my son, and almost every weekend he'd come over. He's really sharp. Taking him back to his house tore me apart. Every time he had a problem, I worried for days. How could I solve things for him when it involved his new stepdad?

"Finally, my ex told me she was moving away (350 miles). I hit the ceiling! I played my trump card. If she went I'd not pay child support! She'd better not take my son away!

"She did. I didn't. And one day the sheriff came and took me to jail!

"So, resigning myself to the inevitable, I tried to maintain contact. Letters and telephone calls were inadequate and became infrequent. I drove up two or three times a year for a weekend and settled for that.

"With my son so far away, I found that I wasn't being torn apart two and three times a week as before. I began to heal and to find a space for other activities and relationships. I grew.

"But no one will replace my son! And, whatever else I have and whomever else I know—I still want his companionship and his love—what father doesn't want this from his only son?

"Seeing him now is so painful that it's a punishment. I don't see him often—or write—or call. I can't stand the pain."

—L. T.

"My wife divorced me and took the kids away. Sure, I've got visitation rights, but they've moved 500 miles away. When am I supposed to see them?"

—T. R.

"I left my wife and kids because I just couldn't stand it anymore. I'd made a mess out of my life and theirs. My wife hated me, and the kids didn't pay any attention to me. I decided everyone'd be better off if I just got out of the picture and let them have a chance at a new life, now that she's remarried."

—K. N.

"If I never see my children again, I'll still be content if I know they are happy and well adjusted."

—J. K.

"I wonder if I should keep visiting my children. Every three or four months I plan a visit, and the kids get all mixed up. One climbs all over me the minute I walk in and then pushes me away. Seems like I just upset things."

—D. P.

"The kids and I always get along ok, but my ex-wife makes me regret each visit by starting a fight the minute I arrive. Things became worse when I remarried. Now, if I go over, I just wait in the car and drop the kids off when we get back. I don't go in!"

—C. V.

"What hurts me the most is that someone else (the stepdad) is raising my son. He shares in those day-to-day experiences which build that solid relationship between a boy and his dad."

—E. L.

Absent Is Not Unloving

The changes in the relationship between children and their noncustodial parents (typically the father, although the trend is slowly changing) vary from family to family. In some families what had been a close relationship becomes a more casual interaction with the loss of daily contact. On the other hand, some children find that they actually have a better relationship with their noncustodial parent because during visitation they pay attention to each other. As one boy put it in a movie about divorce, "When he was married to mom, Dad was too busy for us kids. He always had lists of things to do. But now—we're on the list!"

Perhaps it is most difficult for a parent to maintain a

working relationship with children who live some distance away. Long distance relationships take more work and are less satisfying. Letters are so one-dimensional. Phone calls are either too short or too expensive. Visits take careful planning and coordination. Gifts sent by mail deprive the givers the pleasure of seeing the expressions on the children's faces when they receive the presents.

Visiting the parent who lives several hundred miles away is different than spending every other weekend together. Instead the children stay several weeks, just long enough for everyone to get used to living together again. Then the visit is over. "It tears me apart every time," Nate confesses. "I am depressed for weeks after they leave. Sometimes I wonder if the pleasure of their company is worth the pain of their absence."

People cope with this pain in different ways. Some withdraw from or avoid the source and become absent parents. Some refuse to allow the children to get close enough emotionally to cause pain when they leave. Other people do not always understand or accept the actions of a person who is attempting to cope with the loss of a relationship with a child. But custodial parents need to recognize that absence does not necessarily mean unloving.

I Feel So Bad!

The trauma of a divorce and the subsequent loss of the custody of a child forces a person through a gauntlet of intense emotions.

1. Feelings of loss

Parents who have raised a child from infancy experience a very real sense of loss when the child goes to live with the other parent. Even if the relationship hadn't been all that close, the break underlines and emphasizes the "if only's." Because wanting out of a marriage does not mean wanting to lose the children, some noncustodial parents are left with the feeling of having thrown the baby out with the bathwater.

2. Feelings of rejection

Divorce is the ultimate rejection by someone who has been intimately involved in one's life. When the children go to live with the person doing most of the rejecting, the non-custodial parent may also feel rejected by his offspring.

3. Feelings of guilt

The sources of guilt are as varied as the thoughts of "I should" which plague a person.

—I should have stayed married.

—I should have been a better parent.

—I should have been more patient.

—I should have . . . ad infinitum.

Guilt grabs at and hangs onto blame. Guilt is an imagined parent who stands with one foot on the ego, and unmercifully judges with a yardstick devised by an outside source: parental teachings, society, or a supposedly unreasonable God. Every shortcoming is given a stiff sentence. No witnesses are allowed for the defense. No extenuating circumstances are recognized. Imperfection equates to guilty.

If a spouse fell apart after the divorce, "It's your fault!" Guilt says smugly. (And yet even before the divorce the spouse had been unable to cope.)

If a child begins to fail in school, "It's your fault!" Guilt accuses, ignoring any other causes for the academic problems.

And so guilt finds ways to destroy lives. It keeps people from enjoying the positive aspects of their new life-styles and from adjusting to new realities.

4. Feelings of fear and anger

Facing the reconstruction of their lives after a divorce, noncustodial parents experience many fears. Will their children understand the divorce and still love them? Will the children love the stepparents more than their natural parents? Often these fears are expressed through anger. Inward directed— withdrawal and depression. Or, outward directed—hostility, resentment or violence. Sometimes anger toward the ex-spouse is expressed by not making support payments, or by deliberately not adhering to the agreed upon visitation schedule. Not infrequently the anger is directed toward the justice (or injustice) system which granted custody to the other parent.

5. Feelings of loneliness

Parents without custody who have not yet remarried often find the loneliness unbearable. "I couldn't face coming home after work to an empty apartment," Henry says. "So for the first year or so I scheduled something every evening: church, bowling, tennis, parties, evening college classes. By the time I went home I would be so tired I would just shower and go to bed."

Sometimes parents feel as lonely as the discarded toys waiting for the next visit as expressed in the following poem:

Daddy's House

For twelve days
    in a twelve by twelve closet
    Julietta
    fabric friend
    flop-faced upon
      the Bert and Ernie pillow
    guards rows of
      little tall books
        with
      big short words
    and a tin box
      stuffed
      with secret stuff
Till at each new moon and full
    a little girl
    who ought to live
      here visits
Sunshine glimmers into
    Julietta's brown button eyes
    and pages read
      by dreamlight
      in the night
    warm to loving laughter
      for two days
      twice a month
Then it
    becomes a Waiting Room
    again
        —Leilani Cottingham Collins

6. Feelings of relief and freedom

Mingled with the negative feelings come relief and freedom, although some people deny themselves the right to any positive feelings because they feel guilt about enjoying not having the children.

Philip has come to terms with his situation. "No children means that the house stays straightened all day. The half-gallon of ice cream stays in the freezer until I want it. No rock music or cartoon shows interrupt my Saturday morning sleep-in. Sometimes I feel like a grandparent the way I enjoy the children now. Fun to be with. Fun to send home."

There is no one right way to feel when a person becomes single and loses the custody of the children. Individual responses to the situation depend on past experiences and emotional maturity. Should the negative feelings seem extremely intense or prolonged, perhaps a professional counselor can provide assistance in resolving the pain.

Why Did You Do That?

In expressing negative feelings, people sometimes behave in a manner which seems strange to those who do not see beyond the actions to the pain. People bombarded from within by strong feelings often develop defense or coping mechanisms. For example:

1. Denial of pain

As a way of coping some people simply refuse to admit, even to themselves, that they are feeling any pain. Losing the children didn't hurt.

2. Alienation of others

Some people withdraw from pain by alienating the children. As long as they do not have to be close to, depend on, or answer to any other people, their world is self-controlled and safe. Alienation averts future pain because it prevents vulnerability in relationships.

3. Apathy

Alienation and denial of pain are active responses. Apathy is a passive retreat. Pain is acknowledged, but nothing will be done about it. Apathy characterizes the parent who has given up to the pain.

4. Projection

Sometimes parents who lose custody of their children can only shore up their own self-images by projecting their pain onto others. The children are the ones who are hurting, frustrated, angry, lonely, and mistreated.

5. Physical illnesses

Migraine headaches, ulcers, nervous stomachs, shingles, and many other maladies are often a result of severe emotional stress and pain. Often the physical pain is easier to handle than the emotional pain.

Identifying and accepting one's negative feelings are the first steps to resolving negative behaviors. Through self acceptance and a strong faith in the sovereignty of God, people can learn to rise above the pain in life.

Growing Up Together

Parents who desire to continue to have positive relationships with their children will want to adopt constructive attitudes toward the custodial family.

—Accepting the stepparent as a person who will have a great deal of influence over the children.

—Cooperating with the stepparent as much as possible in raising the children.

Neil did. "When Marcia married Ivan, our son was ten years old and I wondered how he would adjust to having a stepfather. One day about a year later Ivan called me and asked if we could have coffee. He wanted to discuss some problems he was having with David (my son) and to see if I had any suggestions. Although I was surprised, I agreed to meet him. As we talked, I could see that Ivan really cared about David and Marcia. He listened to my ideas and thanked me. Since then we have met several times for similar reasons. While we are not close friends, I do respect and trust him."

—Avoiding "Disneyland visitation" by dividing the time with the children to include everyday chores and activities as well as special treats.

—Maintaining frequent contact with the children.

—Respecting the relationship of the children with their stepparents by not criticizing or belittling them.

—Establishing house rules during visitation while respecting the differences in life-styles at the other home.

—Maintaining open and honest communication with the children.

—Ensuring that the children have a place of their own in the house, so they will feel they are more than visitors—they belong.

The task of being an effective parent when the children live elsewhere is indeed challenging and seldom appreciated. But the investment pays off. Paul reminds us in Galatians 6:9 not to be weary in well-doing, for in time we shall reap our reward.

Chapter Eight
The Parent with Custody

≈ ≳

Parents who have custody of their children and remarry may encounter stressful situations unique to their role.

Adam is troubled. "I feel pulled in both directions. My son, Danny, and I lived alone together for several years before I married Debbie. We had developed a sort of routine: Monday night football on television; Friday nights, sports at his high school (he played, I watched); and Saturdays we ate out for breakfast. After I married Debbie, I realized that she felt left out when Danny and I continued on with our scheduled plans, but when I included Debbie, then Danny felt pushed aside and angry. I also tried to include Danny in any special plans Debbie and I made. That didn't work either. I'm beginning to feel that whenever I talk to or spend time with either Debbie or Danny, the other is resentful and hurt!"

Milly feels as if she were a buffer between her new husband and her children. "I find myself trying to resolve any problem with the children before Harry hears about it so he won't be irritated or think that the kids are nothing but trouble. And on the other hand, I'm always careful to let Harry know when one of the children needs a special hug or compliment. I have the children tell me ahead of time if they are going to ask Harry for something so I can avoid bothering him if I can respond to the request. And in spite of all of my efforts, the children are always complaining to me about Harry; and he often makes disparaging remarks to me about the children. I'm sure if they would all just get to know each other, they could be very good friends! Sometimes I'm so tired of it all."

The Setup

Both Adam and Milly are setting their spouses up for failure. Neither one is allowing the spouse to establish an independent relationship with the stepchild. Adam is allowing Debbie and Danny to compete for his time and attention. Milly is channeling through herself most communication between stepparent and stepchildren. Adam and Milly's instinctively parental desires to keep the peace and to ensure that their spouses and their children get along are having the reverse effect. As difficult as it may often be to see the people one loves the most struggling to live with each other, parents are advised to stay out of the interaction unless physical violence is threatened. Stepparents and stepchildren must build their own relationships in their own time and style. No amount of coaching, forcing, or interfering from the parent will help.

A second setup for which parents are sometimes responsible is overcompensating for the stepparents. Little is gained when parents go to extremes to give their children what the stepparents are withholding—be it money, gifts, attention, or freedoms. By overcompensating, parents undermine the stepparents' authority, credibility, and relationship with the children. Parents are only responsible for their own relationship with their children. The attempt of parents to take responsibility for the stepparents' relationships discounts both the spouses and the children. Some parents feel they must be extra generous to their children because of deep guilt feelings—as if new possessions could compensate for parental failings.

Ruth shared how she used to do things before she learned the secret of forgiveness in relationships. "Whenever I would be too harsh with the children and later feel guilty, I would do something special for them—bake cookies, or take them to the movies. Then one day I realized I wasn't taking care of the real issues. So, the next time I blew it, I sat down with the children and asked for their forgiveness. What a neat blessing! I felt closer to them than ever before! And, I recognized that in doing that, I was modeling the behavior I wanted my kids to learn!"

A third way in which parents tend to set up their spouses for failure is to expect them to view the children with the same loving prejudice as do the parents.

"Wasn't Ginny's solo wonderful?" Fran asked her new husband after the school recital.

"Yes," Lee responded sincerely. "She only missed a couple of notes."

Ginny was hurt. Lee didn't have to be so critical, she thought. Lee, unaware that he had said anything amiss, squeezed Ginny's hand.

Also, looking through the family album at old baby pictures and retelling the young antics of children tends to be much more fascinating to a parent than to a stepparent, who wasn't part of the family back when.

As much as stepparents may love their stepchildren, they may never dote the same way a parent does. That's probably because a stepparent's ego is not directly linked to success or failure in the life of someone else's child. Parents, on the other hand, often feel directly responsible for the success or failure of their children.

Undermining a stepparent's attempts at disciplining can be another setup. Parents are often tempted to "pull rank" when they think a stepparent is being either too lenient or too strict. Most couples who were interviewed agreed that differences in discipline approaches were best discussed privately rather than in front of the children. If, after discussion, the couple decided to change a discipline decision, the adult making the original decision should be the one to communicate the change to the children. Thus the credibility and authority of both adults are preserved.

Of course, should either the parent or the stepparent become excessively violent or abusive with the children, professional assistance is absolutely required. Child abuse is seldom deliberate cruelty but rather a symptom of unresolved psychological pain—usually from being abused as a child. Intensive therapy has proven effective in assisting people to resolve their pain and to learn new behavior for relating to children.

Parents who have custody of their children and who are in the process of building a new family through remarriage will want to be very careful not to set up their spouses for failure.

Opaque Obstacles

Sometimes it is difficult to see through problems to the possible solutions. And yet, when the air is cleared of angry hostilities and frustrations, alternatives can be seen. A few of the types of problems encountered by remarried, custodial parents include:

1. I-love-you,-but-your-children-give-me-a-headache.

Heidi and Frank had this problem. "Frank has never been around children," Heidi says. "He was an only child and never spent much time playing with neighborhood children. Instead, he took piano lessons, practiced faithfully, read a lot of books, and watched television. He was a natural student and never was involved in competitive sports. Because he was charming and attractive, the kids at school all liked him. I think that when we married, he encountered his first experience with sharing. It was an awful shock! He tries, really he does. But he has no idea about how to live with children. We are always fighting. I don't know if we can make it or not. I think about the alternatives: leave Frank; or send the children to live with their father. But I realize that if I let the children break up my marriage, I'd never forgive them. And if I let Frank break up my relationship with my children, I'd never forgive him!"

Some adults do not make good parents or stepparents. Unfortunately there is no qualifying exam as a prerequisite to parenthood. And, until recently, our society did not accept the desire to remain childless. And so most married couples had children, which means that most divorcing couples had children, and consequently most remarrying adults find that children are included in the new family. Hence, there are many opportunities for an adult who finds parenthood an unwanted role, to become, nonetheless, a parent.

Parents whose spouses fit into that category have several options, none of which are ideal. For example,

—Clarence and Ila were quickly divorced.

—Bonnie sent Gary for counseling as a condition of staying married to him.

—Connie tried to ignore the problem.

The best solution is to acknowledge the situation and seek to minimize irritations while the family members learn new ways to relate to one another. People must remember that all behavior is learned, and what has been learned can be unlearned.

2. Effective-immediately-everything-is-going-to-be-different-around here!

When Martin married the housekeeper he had hired to care for his home and five young children after the death of his wife, he thought it was a perfect match. For over a year, Ellie had functioned as a quasi-mother and run the house smoothly. She had slipped easily into the casual atmosphere, quickly befriending the children.

Martin and the children were unhappily surprised when the honeymoon ended abruptly with a complete change in house rules. Now that she was "really" in charge of running the home, Ellie ruled with an iron hand. Rules were strict, punishment swift and severe. Even Martin was expected to become punctual, neat, and helpful around the house. The children were quickly alienated; Martin withdrew from the family and never recovered from the shock. Ellie, refusing to acknowledge that she might have created a problem, suffered the rejection with a martyr's misery, turning to other sources for personal satisfaction.

The immediate and total change of a life-style is too traumatic to impose on a stepfamily. Changes come slowly— one at a time. All family members need to be involved in planning for change.

3. It-isn't-incest-if-we're-not-related.

Sexual attraction may create a problem in stepfamilies. Attraction between various family members:

a. Stepbrothers and stepsisters

Adolescent stepsiblings who have not grown up together may find themselves thrown together in a variety of intimate living situations. Their sexual curiosities and interests already aroused, they may be tempted to "experiment" with each other. Parents will want to establish appropriate house rules. Teenage stepbrothers and sisters should observe the same house rules parents would set for friends of the opposite sex.

b. Stepfathers and stepdaughters

Adolescent girls who bounce around in skimpy nightgowns, or who are extremely physically affectionate with their stepfathers tempt them to carnal fantasies. And sometimes young girls seek to establish their own womanhood by competing with their mothers for the stepfather's attention and affection.

c. Stepmothers and stepsons

Statistics show that divorced men tend to marry women

who are somewhat younger than they. And so the differences in ages between a stepmother and stepson may be less than between the woman and her husband. (For example, a 40-year-old man with a 19-year-old son marries a 28-year-old woman. There are 12 years difference between the man and wife but only 9 years difference between woman and stepson.) And so sexual attractions may develop.

In spite of the fact that sexual relationships between members of a stepfamily are not covered by the incest laws of all states, they are covered by God's laws for chastity and moral purity.

Positive Approaches

The parent who has custody of the children and who is remarried will learn to focus on positive approaches to family life. The first step is keeping Christ at the center of the family. The next step is learning to love family members even as Christ loves the church. This could mean:

—Accepting people where they are in their personal and spiritual development.
—Understanding that every person falls short of God's ideals.
—Listening without judging.
—Agreeing to disagree, when values and opinions are contradictory.
—Cooperating rather than competing or controlling.
—Acknowledging and owning fears, feelings, and insecurities.
—Risking vulnerability.
—Forgiving one another in love.

As the parent enjoys the children and relates to them in a positive way, the stepparent is given a good role model to follow.

When the Stepparent Is at the Other House

Custodial parents often have to cope with their children having a stepparent over whom the parent has no influence—the stepparent at the other house.

Dottie tells of one Christmas that was especially difficult. "When the invitation had come for the children to spend

Christmas with their father, my immediate reaction had been, 'No! Absolutely not!!! But since they received the invitation from a great aunt who had not consulted me ahead of time, I felt trapped into saying yes. The children were so anxious to see their father that I didn't have the courage to say no. As the time of their departure drew nearer, I was so afraid. I wanted the children to go and had made all the reservations, and yet I was afraid. If the money didn't come for the tickets, I knew that after five years of broken promises, the children would never again trust their father. And, what if he didn't realize how much they had grown and changed in five years?

"Steve was not a cute four-year-old any more, but a nine-year-old-boy who couldn't stand inactivity and got into trouble when he was bored. I also wondered if a stepmother who had never had any children could accept my kids. Deeper still was the fear that he wouldn't let them come back after New Year's. He had threatened to take them away from me time and again, and now after all this time, was he going to try? And finally, when the money came and the tickets were actually paid for, I faced my deepest fear—what if they didn't want to come home?

"I remembered all of our struggles—now blown out of proportion in my panic—times when exhausted from work and night school, I was unrelenting and demanding; occasions when John clenched his fists and said, 'You just don't know how to raise sons!' The long list of chores for Carole and John that were necessary just to keep the family running.

"The evening before they left, we had our Christmas together. And as we read the Christmas story and sang a carol, I was filled with a sense of peace. Later that night I told Carole and John how hard it was for me to let them go and yet how glad I was that they were going.

"As I watched the plane leave the ground the next morning, I told the Lord that He would have to take care of them now since they were beyond my care. The next two weeks were the loneliest of my life. Even as I prayed, I worried about the children. When they returned, my fears subsided, for a while. Then I realized that after five years of silence, their dad had reentered their lives with a new wife! Our lives were about to change again."

Children often do find the noncustodial home more

attractive than the custodial home. During the short-term visits to the former spouse the children tend to be the focus of attention and activities, while in the full-time home the children share the attention with all family members. There also tend to be fewer conflicts between adults and children in the noncustodial home, for the children's needs and wants are usually given priority during their visits. And so Dottie's fears that her children might not want to return were not unrealistic.

When the house rules, values, and standards of behavior in the noncustodial homes are in direct opposition to those of the custodial parents, they sometimes find it difficult to comply with visitation orders.

—Kerry's ex-husband turned away from the church and God after their divorce. He then began living with his young girl friend. When the children visit, they do not attend Sunday school or church for the entire summer.

—Hilda's ex-husband is into drugs. By court order, he is to refrain from using them when the children visit. But from casual comments the children have made, Hilda suspects that he doesn't always comply with the court order.

—Stan's ex-wife often gives wild parties on weekends. She allows the children (ages 8 and 10) to attend and to stay up till the wee hours of the morning. Stan disapproves.

—Van's ex-wife now lives in a commune.

—Ron's ex-wife allows the children to stuff themselves on sweets during their visits to her. Ron's dental bills for the children reflect the results.

It is difficult to deliberately send children into a situation which is perceived as potentially harmful to them. And yet children are entitled to know and interact with both of their parents. At best, parents can be sure to give their children a strong spiritual foundation and then uphold them in prayer at all times. The Lord loves each of His children and will care for them far better than we can.

Part Three
Facing
the Challenges

Chapter Nine
Communicating, Confronting and Forgiving

≪⳥ ⳥≫

Conflict!
A pleasure to some,
A challenge to many,
A reality to all!

What Is Conflict?

David Augsburger explains conflict in his book, Caring Enough to Confront. He says that all of us have an inner thrust toward becoming our own, unique selves. In the process we form opinions, make judgments, experiment, and develop a value system. We have many inputs into our decision-making: parental injunctions, instructions from teachers, sermons from spiritual leaders, principles from God's Word, peer pressures, and our own observations and experiences. But, in the final analysis, the choices we make are our own.

When one person's choices or inner thrust runs counter to another person's values or thrust, conflict results. And since none of us is a carbon copy of another, conflict is inevitable. Conflict is neither bad nor good. It is merely an opportunity to interact with another human being. How that interaction is handled is the significant aspect of conflict.

Good management of conflict builds intimacy in a relationship, binding together the partners while allowing each the space to grow.

Poor management of conflict quickly destroys relationships.

Nonmanagement of conflict decreases communications, which minimizes the intimacy, and eventually destroys the relationship.

It All Began When . . .

Sometimes it is difficult to pinpoint the exact cause of a family conflict, and seldom is the contention limited to one issue. Often other factors than the triggering incident influence the hostilities.

—Just before mealtimes, when blood sugars are low, people tend to be less patient with one another.

—Research has proven that laboratory animals who are physically crowded together for extended periods of time, experience anxiety and attack each other frenziedly. People also need sufficient physical space to feel comfortable. So if the home is physically very crowded, some family members may be prone to argue with or "attack" other family members.

—Fears, insecurities, a sense of inadequacy, or being under a lot of stress can cause people to be easily aroused to quarrel.

—Failure to forgive each other for past wrongs builds a foundation of bitterness, resentment, and anger on which new conflicts are easily built.

Nine-year-old Bruce and eleven-year-old Jean were fighting.

Mother: "What's going on here?"
Bruce: "She hit me!"
Jean: "He hit me first!"
Bruce: "She took my records."
Jean: "Because he rode my bike without asking."
Bruce: "So what? Last week she used my radio!"
Jean: "He took it back, so I didn't get to listen to my favorite station!"

Mother held up her hand for silence. Bruce and Jean were getting nowhere by trading grievances. Each accusation merely triggered a counterattack!

How do people clashes start? Always because of differences—

1. In values
2. In ideas
3. In needs
4. In wants

Stepfamily situations are especially open to conflicts for several reasons:

—there are more people in the family structure to interact with and to clash with;

—the noncustodial parent (whose values and opinions may differ from those of the custodial parent) still has some influence over the children;

—the merging of two families is impossible without finding some differences in habits, preferences, or values.

Conflict Styles

People in conflict may choose among five conflict styles: withdraw, win, yield, compromise, or resolve. Each style has a payoff and a cost, as discussed by James G.T. Fairfield in When You Don't Agree.

1. Withdraw

Joyce withdraws. At the first hint of a disagreement she changes the subject, ignores the other person, leaves the room, or the house, or goes to sleep. Temporary withdrawal from a fight to gain control over angry feelings is often an appropriate technique. However, as a predominant method for handling conflict, withdrawal is costly. Consistent withdrawal indicates a giving up on the relationship and on self. By withdrawing, a person says "I don't have enough faith in our relationship to risk a confrontation" Or, "I'll lose anyway, so why argue?"

Over an extended period of time, a person who withdraws from conflict in a relationship begins to turn away psychologically from the other person. Other people and new relationships are sought to fill the void.

The payoff—avoidance of the disagreeableness of an argument or confrontation.

The cost—the lost relationship.

2. Win

Russ cannot bear to lose—a chess game, a tennis match, a discussion, anything. Any competition fires up his desire to win. In the heat of conflict, he loses sight of people, relationships, even issues, as he presses for victory. On those occasions when he doesn't win, Russ becomes almost impossible to live with as he sulks, plans how to get even, or perfects his playing skills for the next game.

Winners seem successful in life because they are usually achievers. But their relationships are superficial and often short-lived. For winning as a consistent style sacrifices the relationship, and victory is achieved at the expense of the other person's ideas, opinions, values, or rights.

The payoff—victory.

The cost—the lost relationship.

3. Yield

"I give up. We'll do it your way." Sean said with a resigned sigh. Not that he still wasn't sure his idea wasn't better for solving the Saturday schedule problem, but rather because it was easier to yield than to continue arguing for hours with Wilma who never gave in. Yielding as a conflict style is not being persuaded to the opponent's point of view but merely going along just to end the discussion.

Yielding does bring peace, and the relationship can continue. However, a relationship in which one person does most of the yielding never has a high level of mutual trust and intimacy. In healthy relationships there is a balance of giving and taking. In a one-sided relationship the giver will not feel very valuable to the taker, whose victories are at the giver's expense.

The payoff—peace, and a continued relationship.

The cost—a one-sided relationship in which one's self-esteem is diminished.

4. Compromise

In a compromise, each person gives in a little so that the conflict is resolved without either person being **THE** winner or **THE** loser. But each person wins a little and each loses a little. The fact that both parties are willing to compromise indicates that they consider their relationship to be more important than their differences.

The payoff—a good relationship and an acceptable resolution to an issue.

The cost—not achieving one's goals which are sometimes too important to be compromised.

5. Resolve

The most ideal style, and the one which takes the most work, is to resolve conflicts. Partners (siblings, spouses, or friends) agree that they have a difference of opinion and work together to develop the best possible solution. Several alternatives are explored. Pros and cons are discussed. Neither person claims a specific alternative as his own to be sold, defended, or sacrificed. The costs and payoffs of each are weighed, and the final choice is the one both people believe to be the best solution.

The resolve style acknowledges the importance of both the relationship and the issue without sacrificing either one. The solution belongs to both partners because they developed it together. And the joint investment of creative energy to resolve a problem brings increased intimacy to the relationship. The resolve style gives each party an equal status for the purpose of resolving the conflict, even if one party has some authority over the other. For example, a parent and a child could use this style without parental authority being used to influence the final decision.

The resolve style requires a great deal of time, energy, and emotional investment, so it is not practical for every family conflict. However, for the major issues, the best method is to resolve the conflict.

The payoff—an improved relationship, and a good solution to the problem.

The cost—time, energy, and emotional investment.

Most people use each of the above styles in their day-to-day confrontations with different people. The style selected is the one deemed to be the most workable in a given situation. Conflict styles are developed during childhood by observing behaviors which were successful for others, and by experimenting with one's family members. Relational styles are modified as people grow up, select values, respond to peer pressures and have increased experiences with trial and error. Some people never evaluate their conflict styles and thus never make a conscious effort to improve their interactions. Others, people who are into growing and developing as human beings, are always evaluating, seeking feedback, and making positive life changes.

The Ideal Role Model

As human beings, we are often in conflict with God, and His behavior toward us serves as a beautiful role model for us.

—He did not **withdraw** from us. "But God commendeth His love toward us, in that, while we were yet sinners, Christ died for us." Romans 5:8

—He did not **win** over us by flaunting His holiness and condemning our sinful selves. "For God sent not His Son into the world to condemn the world; but that the world through Him might be saved." John 3:17

—He does not **yield** to our sinful rebellion against His righteousness. But "he that believeth not is condemned already, because he hath not believed in the name of the only-begotten Son of God." John 3:18

—He does not **compromise** His plans. "Jesus saith unto him, I am the Way, the Truth, and the Life; no man cometh unto the Father but by Me." John 14:6

—He does **resolve** our problems with us. "Come now, and let us reason together, saith the Lord: though your sins be as scarlet, they shall be as white as snow; though they be red like crimson, they shall be as wool." Isaiah 1:18

Forgiveness Comes First

The whole basis of our relationship with God is that He loves us enough to forgive our sins and accept us where we are. We do not deserve to be forgiven; we ought to pay full penalty for our sins, but to do so would cut us off from God in an eternal hell. So God provided a substitute for our punishment when He allowed His own Son to take upon Himself the sins of the world and die on the cross for us. Through His sacrifice we are made whole, that is, we are given perfect status in the body of Christ and fully justified so as to be able to enter an eternal heaven.

Each daily transgression, sin, or failing is freely forgiven as we come repentant to the Father in prayer. He loves us enough, as He promised, to forgive us always. "If we confess our sins, He is faithful and just to forgive us our sins and to cleanse us from all unrighteousness." 1 John 1:9

Experiencing God's healing forgiveness after we have sinned is a wonderful restorative to a wounded spirit. It is fantastic!

The hard part is translating that same forgiveness to others—which is exactly what God expects of us. In Ephesians 4:32 and Colossians 3:13 we are told to forgive others even as Christ has forgiven us. And yet we cannot humanly achieve this ideal. We can only learn to be truly forgiving with God's help and in His strength. People having difficulty in forgiving others will want to read David Augsburger's book, The Freedom of Forgiveness (Moody Press, 1970).

In his book, David Augsburger says that forgiveness is rare, hard, costly, and substitutional. Rare because it is hard and costly.

Hard because in refusing to insist on one's rights when unjustly wronged by another, one chooses to suffer undeservedly.

Costly because the offender goes free while the offended suffers hurt or loss without restitution.

Substitutional because in forgiving another, responsibility for the pain is assumed by the forgiving person.

Forgiveness is not something to be withheld until it has been earned through confession, restitution, or suffering. Forgiveness is a free and undeserved pardon. That's how God forgives us and how we are to forgive others.

The cost of forgiving is high, but the cost of not forgiving is even higher. For not to forgive is to be filled with unresolved anger, resentments, and bitterness, which in turn disallow inner peace and joy.

But the most important reason for forgiving is found in Matthew 6:14, 15: "For if ye forgive men their trespasses, your heavenly Father will also forgive you: But if ye forgive not men their trespasses, neither will your Father forgive your trespasses."

A forgiving attitude towards others facilitates the process of conflict resolution, for in order to be able to forgive, one must be able to accept people where they are. People are not perfect, they are in the process of becoming, as illustrated in the following poem.

The Age of Becoming

I have arrived at the age of becoming.
No longer do I face the fear
Of what I shall be
When I grow up.
I am becoming.
I see my armor chinks
For what they are—
Pressure points created by the stress of living.

Not permanent but changing.
I am becoming.
Relationships are not locked in—
But open,
Free to change
As life and time bring growth
To each of us—
In different ways.
We are becoming.

—by Dottie Williams

Because people are in the process of becoming, they are sometimes thoughtless and cruel to one another. Only through forgiveness of one another can relationships survive and grow. Forgiveness lets go of the hurt and disappointments and restores the trust to the relationship by allowing each person to be himself, an imperfect human being.

As we remember that we ourselves are forgiven, imperfect transgressors of God's laws, we can more easily reach out in forgiveness to those who violate our expectations for them. We can accept ourselves and others as people-in-progress. We are all growing. We all make wrong decisions or choices in the growing process, but through forgiveness we are free to venture out in new efforts to grow into the image of Christ.

Assuming Responsibility

Assertively assuming the responsibility for one's own behavior and feelings is essential for free and creative relationships. People choose who they are and how they will behave. Sometimes it seems that there are no choices and that someone else is in control of the situation—but there is always a choice! Granted, sometimes all of the choices are negative! An armed robber demands money. The victim chooses either to hand over the money or to refuse and risk being shot. Two negative alternatives, but choices nonetheless!

So, people have choices about how they will relate to other people, whether to hold grudges, to forgive, to love, or to hate.

Communicating Effectively

Accurately transmitting an exact message from one

person to another is a complicated process. Thoughts, feelings, and concepts are translated into words and relayed from the source to the receiver, who then decodes the message from mere words back into thoughts, feelings, and concepts. However, in each transmission, some of the precise meanings are distorted or lost. Words have specific meanings to people based on their total life experiences with the words. Therefore, when a particular word is used, it often has different meanings to different people. Learning to communicate clearly with others requires paying more attention than usual to what is said and how it is received.

Sending a clear message includes:
—Knowing exactly what is to be communicated;
—Organizing thoughts into a logical sequence;
—Selecting precise words to express ideas;
—Using concrete instead of abstract words;
—Soliciting frequent feedback to determine if the message was received as it was sent.

Receiving a clear message includes:
—Listening for meanings behind the words;
—Refraining from composing a response while the other person is still speaking;
—Giving feedback to the speaker to ensure that the message received was what was sent;
—Responding to the person, and the message, even if the communicating skills are poor.

Learning to communicate effectively with the members of one's family is perhaps the ultimate challenge. Day-to-day living in the same house does not ensure that people listen to or accept one another.

"If he really loved me, he would want to go to the symphony with me. I watch football on television with him!" Nellie wails.

"If she really loved me," Keith responds, "she wouldn't want me to sit through something I hate! She doesn't have to watch football with me—she can go do something else!"

Message sent was not message received.

Scarcely recognizing her own voice, Jenny shrieked, "You will vacuum the rug right now!"

Fourteen-year-old Michael stormed to his room yelling over his shoulder, "I won't, and you can't make me!"

Helplessly aware that Michael was right, Jenny sank into a nearby chair. "I blew it again," she thought. "When am I ever going to handle these confrontations with my stepson? Half of the time I'm rational, but the rest of the time I lose control and scream!"

Breaking a lifetime habit of fighting unfairly is difficult—but not impossible! Changing habits is a slow process. A new behavior is selected and practiced. Sometimes it is used, but at other times the old style surfaces and we slip back into old ways. Earl H. Gaulke's book, You Can Have a Family Where Everybody Wins, is an excellent guide to resolving specific family conflicts in a very positive manner.

Let Not the Sun Go Down

As a teenager on the mission field of Brazil, I lived with a tribe of uncivilized Indians—the Chavantes. And yet, uneducated as they were, these Indians had learned one of God's principles for conflict resolution—"Let not the sun go down upon your wrath" (Ephesians 4:26). Going to bed angry in the Chavante tribe often meant that one of the opponents did not live through the night, taking the life of an enemy being acceptable behavior. However, to prevent the men from killing each other off, the tribe had a solution. Each night before bedtime, the chief would take his grass mat and walk to the center of the village. At his signal, all of the men in the tribe would bring their mats and join the chief, forming a large circle. The chief would then lead a sort of group discussion about any problems that had come up during the day and were still unresolved. All of the men could offer advice to those who were angry with each other. But the council meeting continued until all of the problems were resolved to the satisfaction of those involved.

Sometimes the solutions were unexpectedly creative. I remember once when the corn crops were not yet ready for harvesting and a major problem arose. The women were going into each other's gardens and plucking the tiny ears of corn to serve as delicacies for their husbands. Consequently the corn crop was in serious danger of never maturing. Hours of discussion at the council one night resulted in the perfect solution. Leaving one old man and a couple of children behind in the village to guard the crops, the entire tribe left the next morning for a 6 week hunting trip until the corn ripened!

We too can be creative as we care enough to confront, communicate, and forgive one another.

Conflict?

A difference of values, ideas, wants, or needs.

An opportunity to invest in the life of another person by resolving things together.

A chance to grow.

To love.

For Further Reading

David Augsburger. Caring Enough to Confront (Glendale, CA: Regal Books, 1974)

David Augsburger. The Freedom of Forgiveness (Chicago, IL: Moody Press, 1970)

James G. T. Fairfield. When You Don't Agree (Scottdale, PA: Herald Press, 1977)

Earl H. Gaulke, You Can Have a Family Where Everybody Wins (St. Louis, MO: Concordia Publishing House, 1975)

Rex Johnson, Communication—Key to Your Parents (Irvine, CA: Harvest House Publishers, 1978)

Bruce Narramore, and Bill Counts, Freedom from Guilt (Santa Ana, CA: Vision House Publishers, 1974)

Dave and Jan Stoop, The Total(ed) Parent (Irvine: CA: Harvest House Publishers, 1978)

Norman Wright, An Answer to Family Communication (Irvine, CA: Harvest House Publishers, 1977)

Norman Wright, and Rex Johnson, Communication—Key to Your Teens (Irvine, CA: Harvest House, 1978)

Chapter Ten
Finding Equal Time

≈૨ ૬≈

The precious commodity of time seems even more valuable and treasured in the stepfamily. A quick review of personal demands shows why.

In a first marriage the time demands for interaction or time alone are many:

Needing time alone are:
  1. Mom.
  2. Dad.
  3. The child.

Needing time alone with God are:
  4. Mom.
  5. Dad.
  6. The child.

Needing time alone together are:
  7. Mom and Dad.
  8. Mom and child.
  9. Dad and child.

(NOTE: Repeat 3, 6, 8, and 9 for each child in the family)

These demands are far exceeded in stepfamilies. Consider a family where both spouses have one child from a previous marriage and one child together. The demands for time alone now look like this:

Needing time alone are:
  1. Wife.
  2. Husband.
  3. The child (hers).
  4. The child (his).
  5. The child (theirs).

Needing time alone with God are:
  6. Wife with God.

7. Husband with God.
8. Child (hers) with God.
9. Child (his) with God.
10. Child (theirs) with God.

Needing time alone together are:

11. Wife and husband.
12. Wife and child (hers).
13. Wife and child (his).
14. Wife and child (theirs).
15. Wife and all children.
16. Husband and child (hers).
17. Husband and child (his).
18. Husband and child (theirs).
19. Husband and all children.
20. Wife and husband and all children.
21. Wife and husband and child (his).
22. Wife and husband and child (hers).
23. Wife and husband and child (theirs).
24. Child (hers) with natural father.
25. Child (his) with natural mother.

(Note: If either spouse, or the couple together, has more than one child, the number of demands increase accordingly. At a minimum the demands would increase by five—

1. Time alone
2. Time with God
3. Time with the parent
4. Time with the stepparent
5. Time with the parent and stepparent)

It is no wonder that stepfamilies are so rushed and pressed for time!

How Much Time Is Available?

Not much!

A typical schedule for an adult who works outside the home goes something like this:

AM			
12:00— 6:15	sleep	6.25 hours
6:15— 6:45	personal grooming	.50 hours
6:45— 7:15	breakfast	.50 hours
7:15— 8:00	driving to work	.75 hours
8:00—12:00	work	4.00 hours

PM	12:00— 1:00	lunch	1.00 hours
	1:00— 5:00	work	4.00 hours
	5:00— 5:45	driving home from work	.75 hours
	5:45— 6:15	preparing supper	.50 hours
	6:15— 6:45	supper	.50 hours
	6:45— 8:00	general housekeeping, maintenance chores	1.25 hours
	8:00—10:00	family time	2.00 hours
	10:00—10:30	personal grooming	.50 hours
	10:30—12:00	"FREE" TIME!	1.50 hours
		TOTAL	24.00 hours

It is no coincidence that family time coincides with television's prime-time periods, because advertisers know that working parents often find themselves too tired in the evenings to do much more than watch television with their families. Couples whose time alone together is the leftover one and one-half hours at the end of a very busy day, often find it difficult to share on a deep personal level with one another.

Creative Scheduling

The solution is to go creative! Suggestions gathered from various sources—mostly people living in step—are presented below, roughly grouped by the basic categories on the typical schedule given above.

1. Sleeptime

Janet sacrifices an hour of her sleeptime two or three times a week to get up early and be alone. Taking her cup of coffee to the patio (except in winter when she sits in front of a fire in the fireplace), she spends time getting in touch with herself and sifting through her thoughts. She admits that often having made the extra effort to get away from her family, she frequently finds herself thinking about each member and experiencing a rush of love for each one.

—Smitty also gets up early to jog.

—Max runs.

—Sally reads the newspaper.

—Ed (and many others) has his personal devotions.

—Cathy goes to work early to beat the traffic.

—Elmer, who works at home, lies awake in bed savoring the solitude until everyone else has left the house for the day.

2. Personal grooming time (AM or PM)

—Peggy cherishes those early morning minutes with hubby Richard. As he shaves, showers, and dresses for work, they discuss their individual and mutual plans for the day. "Starting the day together," Peggy says thoughtfully, "has been something precious to look forward to and back on, regardless of what happens during the day."

—Judy retreats to soak in the tub, luxuriating in the warm quietness where she won't be called upon to resolve filial disputes.

—Husband Howard and wife Sherry love to shower together.

—Marilyn and daughter Christine share a bathroom for morning make-up application sessions and girl talk while husband Joe and son Andy share the second bathroom. "It's kind of fun shaving with your son," Joe grins, "but what is more important is that we also talk. Sometimes it's just small talk and kidding around, but often we discuss very important issues."

3. Breakfast or supper

Breakfast traditions range from the get-your-own-when-you-want-it, to the you-don't-leave-until-you've-had-your-hot-breakfast beliefs. Supper is traditionally a family meal.

But the creative stepfamily, eager to find time for everyone, will want to evaluate traditions and choose their own habits carefully.

—Becky skips breakfast so she can have time alone.

—Jerry has personal devotions instead of breakfast.

—The Johnsons (who have teenagers) find that breakfast is the one time when all family members are most likely to be together, so they have turned it into a sharing time. Plans or problems are discussed, and a brief family worship is held before everyone leaves for the day.

—Dorothy has breakfast alone with 19-year-old son Al, before the rest of the family gets up.

—The Campbells plan a once-a-month Saturday breakfast celebration by eating out in a favorite restaurant.

—Martha squeezes in time alone by snacking while preparing supper, then going to the bedroom alone to read, watch television, or work on a project while the rest of the family eats supper.

—Duane and Yolanda often use suppertime to be alone with his children. Yolanda takes Dawn out to eat (a special treat for Dawn) while Duane stays home with Grace for sandwiches and a chess game.

—Lauri sometimes serves the children an early supper so she and Kevin can have a quiet mealtime alone when he gets home from work.

4. Driving to (and from) work

—Patrick advocates the one-person-one-car tradition for driving to and from work. "Sometimes I feel it is the last place I can be alone," he says. "On the way to work, I plan the day. On my way home, I prepare to forget the job and spend time with my family."

—Elaine rides the bus so she will have a few minutes each day to read and study the Word of God.

—Marie drives daughter Dolores to school on the way to work so they can spend time sharing.

—Leilani and Jim talk as they ride to work together.

—Billie stays an hour after work to beat the Los Angeles traffic—and still gets home at the same time as if she had left right after work. She has "found" five hours a week this way, which she wisely uses to write letters, read, have personal devotions, make telephone calls, and to be alone.

5. Worktime

The normal eight-hour workday includes at least two 15-minute breaks. People who are serious about redeeming every precious minute will have already discovered these break periods and put them to good use. The most common ideas were: writing letters, studying, doing homework, reading, having personal devotions, making personal phone calls, writing lists of things to do later, planning upcoming events, or working on a hobby such as crocheting, rug hooking, or model building. A very good suggestion is to use at least one of those breaks to do physical relaxation exercises that actually give renewed physical strength and endurance.

6. Lunchtime

—Lynne takes a college class on her lunch hour.

—Tommy writes magazine articles.

—Sharon runs.

—Eileen does homework from her college class.

—Lucy runs errands.

—Dale sleeps.

—Gail and Alex lunch together.

Reading, personal devotions, and some of the other individual activities listed under other categories are also appropriate at lunchtime.

7. Preparing supper or general housekeeping chores

Chores, even the really boring or disagreeable ones, can provide interaction time, because doing chores together can be fun, especially with a little friendly competition like racing to see who finishes first. Talking while working, even complaining to a sympathetic ear, can make the work seem easier. Other creative suggestions included:

—The Wilsons do a thorough housecleaning on weekends and the absolute minimum of cleaning work during the week, so the daily time required for maintenance and housecleaning is minimized, which leaves time for other things.

—The Reeves do just the opposite. Each day, from Monday through Friday, they do a specific part of the overall cleaning and maintenance work so that by Friday night all of the weekly chores are done and the weekend is free for relaxation and individual projects.

Many stepfamilies have learned to rotate the division of regular, routine chores so that the interaction varies from week to week as different members work together on various jobs.

Grocery shopping, running errands, doing the wash at the laundromat, and shopping for clothes are examples of chores that can be done by either parent with one or more of the children, by one person alone, or by the couple.

8. Family time

The concern for family time is for the quality, not just the quantity of interaction. Just being together, while often fun, is not enough. Are there problems to discuss? Plans to be made? Working on a project together can bring people into a greater degree of intimacy than can just watching television together.

Family time is a good opportunity to plan for a variety of family member combinations. For example,

Mondays: Dad and one or more children do something

together while Mom and the rest of the children work on a project. (The same children are not always paired with the same parent.)

Tuesdays: Dad takes the children out to some activity while Mom has time alone.

Wednesdays: Mom and the children get involved in an activity to give Dad time alone.

Thursdays: The whole family spends time together.

Fridays: Mom and Dad go out alone together while the children make other plans.

Basically the 24-hour day is adequate to meet the time demands, but careful planning and scheduling is needed.

Yes, But . . .

Most people agree in concept that there is enough time, but not in practice. Excuses for not having enough time range from tiredness to interruptions, from illness to a change of priorities. The truth is that few people are organized enough in their personal lives to redeem the time.

Basics of Time Management

The basic principles of time management can be applied to the stepfamily's time schedule.

1. First, the priorities for investing time are listed (individually or as a family).

2. Next, all the ways the family spends time during a normal week are listed and the usual amount of time involved computed for each item listed.

3. A third list is developed of things which the family or individuals want to do but have not yet found the time for during a normal week.

4. A comparison of the lists will usually show that many of the time-consuming activities and some of the desired activities do not relate to the priorities on the first list. These discrepancies should be noted. Whenever possible, activities which do not relate to the family priorities should be phased out of the schedule.

—Glenn decided to resign from the Community Action Club he had served on for three years in order to have time to attend his son's Little League baseball games.

—Estelle decided that four years as a girl scout leader was enough, so she opted to take an evening course in child psychology.

5. God's guidance should be sought as a workable new schedule is outlined—in pencil so that needed changes can be made easily. Hourly schedule books are available from any stationery store. The new schedule must be realistic and practical.

First, the routine activities are sketched in: work, church, meetings. Then in priority order, other activities are included, ensuring that interaction time for all family members is included.

6. Living by a schedule is much more difficult than developing one! But within reason the schedule should be followed. Extreme rigidity and inflexibility allows the schedule to run the family—which doesn't work! Rather, the schedule is to be a tool for effectively managing time.

When considering canceling a planned activity because the mood isn't right or they don't feel like following through, people will want to evaluate the impact of changing the schedule. Substituting an alternate activity of equal priority and payoff as the canceled activity is preferable to canceling an activity to sit around doing nothing. When the planned schedule is committed to God, families find that they make fewer modifications to the plans.

7. Each evening the schedule for the following day is reviewed. Needed equipment or supplies are gathered and preparations made so that the planned activities can take place.

8. A sensitivity to God's leading is essential so that outside interruptions are handled appropriately. For example, Dennis may have a two-hour block of time set aside for a project of his own. Then he is asked by Mark, a neighbor, to drive him to the hospital because Mark's wife was just in a car accident. Or, Art calls and wants to discuss a business proposition. Or James and Leslie want him to go out to dinner with them. How should Dennis respond to requests such as these?

Actually there are four choices for responding to interruptions:

a. Ignore the request. Don't answer the telephone or doorbell or open the mail when busy with other tasks. This is difficult to do, besides ignoring friends does not make a positive contribution to the relationship.

b. Postpone the interruption. Ask if the person can call or come back later, at a time agreed upon by both parties.

c. Delegate the interruption to someone else who can deal with the issues.

d. Stop the planned activity and resolve the interruption.

9. Unschedule free time should be used wisely. When a meeting or other activity is unexpectedly canceled by the other people involved, the free time can be filled with reading, writing, planning, telephoning, running errands, or other worthwhile activities.

10. Rescheduling things which did not get accomplished is important. Sometimes a leftover activity will need to receive top priority the next day; however, at other times the need was for a specific day, so it cannot be rescheduled.

Final Reminders

When structuring a workable schedule, family members will find that every person will not have priority every day. However, during a whole week, there will be time for everyone, which makes it easier to accept not getting one's way. For example, 10-year-old Julie, who loves to have her parents play table games with her, is more understanding of their doing other things if she sees that time on the schedule has been set aside for her desires.

When first learning to live on a schedule, people sometimes go overboard and plan activities so close together that the slightest variance upsets the schedule for the rest of the day. This can lead to frustration and the abandonment of the schedule. Few people can suddenly start scheduling their time and not encounter initial setbacks. Time management is a skill requiring the juggling of many variables and is not learned overnight.

Letting feelings or moods determine whether or not the schedule will be followed will eventually undermine the whole process. On Sunday afternoon when the week's plan is developed, Thursday evening may seem the perfect time to sew—or clean the garage. By Thursday, even if sewing and cleaning are the last things they feel like doing, people should follow the plan and then reward their efforts with a special treat.

Since each item listed on a plan is in essence a minigoal, the schedule becomes a list of achievements as each item is completed and crossed off.

Although all of the relationships in the family are important, three are absolute top priorities if the stepfamily is to succeed: time with the Lord, time alone, and time with the spouse. Putting each other first does not cheat the children, for research studies have shown that children tend to be better adjusted human beings if the adults in the home have a good, intimate relationship.

"The strength of our relationship comes from our being there for each other. We couldn't make it if we didn't draw on one another," Dean comments with deep conviction as he smiles at wife Gloria.

A concert pianist once commented that he had to practice playing the piano every day to maintain his skills. If he missed one day, he could detect the difference. If he skipped two days, his critics noticed the change. And after three days of not practicing, his public could hear a difference in his music.

The same principles apply to the intimate relationships between a person and the Lord, and the spouse.

"If I don't get to share with Dean for one whole day I miss him, and I feel unfinished. The change in our relationship becomes noticeable to our children and friends if Dean and I don't share for several days," Gloria says. "It's just that we're so close that space between us is very visible!"

The space between people and the Lord is even more visible to outsiders because in the Lord's strength we are more than conquerors (Romans 8:37), but in our own strength we often let life's problems get us down.

In stepfamilies, time is one precious commodity which cannot be taken for granted or wasted. Carefully rationed, there is enough for everyone, but creative alternatives must be sought to stretch out the hours.

Chapter Eleven
Resolving the Legalities

$\prec \!\! \epsilon \!\! \varrho \quad \varrho \!\! \epsilon \!\! \succ$

When a marriage is legally terminated in court (by divorce or dissolution), there are inevitable "legal leftovers" that force the parties to continue relating to one another, for example, custody and visitation of the children and support payments.

Custody Issues

Custody of minor children has traditionally been awarded to the mother, while the father is usually granted reasonable visitation and ordered to make support payments. This nearly automatic division is in part based on the following concepts: (1) Women are more nurturing than are men; (2) Women are at home most of the time so can provide more stability than a man who must work out of the home for several hours a day; and (3) Men earn more than women and therefore must contribute to the support of the children.

While these concepts are nearly antiquated, little has been done to significantly change trends in court orders regarding custody of minor children. Some states do have laws which mandate that children be awarded to "the most responsible party," but individual judges often interpret that to mean the mother.

Mothers usually expect and want to have custody of their minor children, since our society says this is what "ought to be." However, sometimes a women is candid and honest enough to consider her alternatives. She can assert her equal right to choose whether or not to request custody rather than accepting it as a matter of course. A woman relinquishing custody usually has weighed the situation carefully before making such a serious decision. Her spouse may have more earning power than she. If he has worked longer in his career and has a more secure and stable income, he may be more able to provide for the children. She may feel that she would have a better chance to restructure her life (get her college degree or take a better job) if she does not have the children in her home on a full-time basis. Perhaps if her children are boys (especially teenagers), they have a greater need for their father than their mother in the custodial home.

Even when all of the rational facts indicate that custody of the minor children should be awarded to the father, many women find it difficult if not impossible to relinquish their children. However, more and more women are seeking counseling to assist them in emotionally coping with what is a logically sound decision.

Fathers often do desire custody of their children at the time of the divorce but, unless the mothers agree, their chances are slim. Fathers must prove to the court that they are the better parent, which then implies that the mother is unfit, mentally or morally. Many men, recognizing that they do not have a good chance of winning custody over the objections of their wives, do not make custody a major issue in their divorces. Sometimes they plan to reopen the issue at a later date.

A subsequent change of custody is possible if both parties can agree on the terms. If, however, the noncustodial parent initiates a change of custody action a year or more after the divorce and it is contested by the custodial parent, a change is rare because the children are considered to have made an adjustment to the new home situation.

An attempt at resolving these issues by making shared legal custody the law is supported by many professionals in the counseling fields, attorneys, for example, such organizations as Equal Rights for Fathers, and The Stepfamily Foundation. (See Appendix A for information on these and other resource organizations.)

Visitation Issues

"Reasonable visitation" is generally granted to the non-custodial parent. Whenever possible, the details are left up to the parties involved, but in some cases visitation orders are specified.

Specified visitation orders for a parent who lives close to

the children usually (1) includes every other weekend and (2) dividing up the long school holidays—Christmas and Easter.

For long distance parents, the order might include: (1) one week of the Christmas school vacation; (2) part of the Easter school vacation; and (3) four to five weeks during the summer.

The court encourages parents to be flexible enough to accommodate the needs and desires of both parents and children rather than rigidly enforcing strict adherence to the order.

Support Issues

Noncustodial fathers are typically ordered to make support payments; the amount is computed on their ability to pay and the needs and life-style of the children. Failure to make support payments ordered by the court may result in arrest and imprisonment if the custodial parent files a complaint and presses charges. The process, however, is long and complicated, especially if the defendant lives out of state.

Stepfamily Ramifications

Legal issues left over from a previous marriage become more complex when one (or both) of the parents remarries, because more people are involved.

—A noncustodial parent settling into a new marriage may want to include the children as permanent members of the family. Often this is an attempt to blot out the failure of the first marriage with the image of a complete family unit. Sometimes in remarrying, parents feel that they have more stability and capability of raising children than they did before. Or some parents (usually fathers) believe that in establishing a two-parent home, they now have a better chance at being awarded custody. So a change of custody is requested.

—Custody can be an unanticipated surprise, as in Pauline's case. She was 40 years old at the time of her marriage to Andrew, whose teenage sons lived with their mother. Scarcely three months after their marriage she and Andrew were surprised when all three boys came to live with them, with less than two weeks' notice. "The adjustment period was rough," Pauline confesses. "We hadn't planned for it!"

—Visitation may become a problem if the relationship

between spouses becomes strained when one remarries.

—A man who receives support payments from the father of his stepchildren may have mixed feelings about the money, even while acknowledging that a father has financial responsibility for his children. The stepfather may feel vaguely uneasy about not assuming full responsibility for the woman he married—including her children.

—Noncustodial parents who had been prone to providing financial support above that ordered by the court (for such things as vacations, presents, dental, or medical bills, or large purchases for the home) often encounter some resistance from a new spouse if the extras cause a hardship on the family budget.

Stepparent-Stepchild Legalities

Often questions of adoption or inheritance are raised in steprelationships.

1. What about adoption?

The professional camps are divided with excellent attorneys and counselors on each side. Some are for adoption; others are not. All agree that each case is uniquely individual, and that the reasons for the adoption determine the appropriateness of the action. A summary of opinions follows:

—Yes. Adoption is a sign to the children that the stepparent considers them part of the family.

—No. A commitment is more than a name change. It is a way of life communicated by action.

—Yes. Adoption gives the adopted (step)child equal inheritance rights with the biological children.

—No. A well-written, very specific will can prevent inheritance problems.

—Yes. If the natural parent wants to sign away the responsibilities of children.

—Yes. If the children are very young, and the natural parent (1) is far away and does not plan to keep in touch with the children; (2) does not object, or (3) is deceased.

—No. If the children object.

—No. If the new marriage does not last, the adopted (step)parent will have continued responsibilities for the adopted (step)child.

—Yes. If the marriage does not last, a stepparent has no rights to the "ex" stepchildren.

—No. If the motives are to cut the other parent out of the children's lives from a position of bitterness, anger, vengeance or other negative emotions.

Besides people seem to have an inner drive to unravel the fascinating mystery of their biological roots. So, by the late teens (if not earlier) adopted adolescents often desire contact with their natural parents, so they can understand the missing piece of their life puzzle. This desire for interaction with the natural parent has little to do with the relationship of the child and his adopted (step)parent. It seems common with people who had very happy experiences and strong bonds of love and affection with their adopted (step)parents, as well as those who have had negative experiences.

Strange situations have grown out of the adoption issues. Lance adopted Jo's two-year-old son when they were married. Seven years later when they divorced, Lance requested and was awarded custody of not only Loraine (his and Jo's daughter) but also Robbie, his adopted (step)son.

As with most of life's major decisions, adoption has certain pros and cons that each couple must weigh. Motives are a key concern. People find it easy to justify their own desires by rationalizing that these choices are in the best interest of the children. Often the objective feedback available from a qualified counselor and attorney is of the most help in making a wise decision. Unfortunately there are no clear-cut solutions for individual situations, only several imperfect alternatives with both advantages and disadvantages.

2. What about inheritance?

In most states, stepchildren have no inheritance rights. Therefore stepparents wishing to leave something to their stepchildren will want to write a very specific will and testament so that their desires are carried out.

Opal shared her story. She had been raised by her stepmother from the age of three and had always had a close loving relationship. The stepmother's own daughter, Leann, 20 years older than Opal, had left home at 19, and although she only lived 50 miles away, never contacted her mother. When the stepmother became seriously ill, Opal nursed her through the last five long years of her life. Because there was no will, Leann inherited everything: the house, the small savings, and the car, even though her mother had always said these things were Opal's inheritance.

Since no one knows just when death will come, it is important to have a valid will prepared.

Emotional Merry-Go-Round

One of the basic reasons that custody, visitation, support, adoption, and inheritance are legal issues is that people get caught in a whirl of conflicting feelings when confronted with these issues. Objective third party intervention is often needed to keep the child's best interest in sight (or in the case of inheritance, to follow through with the desires of the deceased). Sometimes our legal system works that miracle and sometimes it fails, but at this time a better alternative is not available, although several are being proposed such as shared custody and taking custody and visitations out of the court system.

Children also get caught on the emotional merry-go-round when their parents fight over custody, visitation, or support issues. The two most important people in their lives are opponents and the children are the prize! Some children gain a sense of personal power and importance to be the cause of such major confrontation. Some children take sides. Some turn to people outside the family for the peace and stability they desire.

Just how open parents should be with their children regarding the legal disagreements will depend on the age and emotional maturity of the children and the impact such knowledge would have on their lives. Calmly and factually answering questions without putting down the character of the other parent is usually a safe approach. Sharing all of one's inner ugliness, the anger, the fears, and insisting that the children agree is usually a destructive approach.

Proceed with Caution!

First and foremost: Don't play legal games! Issues serious enough to require a court decision are not to be handled lightly. Using an attorney or the court simply for a show of power is childish and irresponsible. In fact, a good attorney will urge the parties to work through conflicts without going to court.

Secondly, don't use the court to resolve feelings of guilt, anger, or fear. A woman who is willing for her children to live with their father but makes him take them away through a court battle so that she won't feel guilty at having deserted them has wasted everyone's time and money. She will probably still carry the guilt until she comes to terms with and accepts her desires. A person who tries to use the court to punish an ex-spouse in some way often finds that the children are the ones who suffer the most.

Our court system being what it is, family law cases are often decided in a vacuum of information. A business case involving several thousand dollars may take days to resolve in court while family law cases are scheduled 10—15 minutes apart. One lawyer reported that 80 percent of his city's court cases involved family law, yet only 12 percent of the court resources were allocated for those cases! It become obvious that court decisions are not always going to be perfect.

People considering initiating legal actions toward an ex-spouse regarding custody, visitation, or support will want to have answered the following questions to their own satisfaction.

1. Motives

Am I trying to do what's best for my children or for myself? Am I planning to use the courtroom arena to display my strength or to prove a point? Am I angry, bitter, hostile, or vindictive toward my ex-spouse? Do I feel this legal action will be a vehicle for expressing those feelings? Am I afraid? What are my real motives?

2. Alternatives

Have I considered every other alternative? Is there any other way to resolve this problem? Am I sure that the advantages of taking this matter to court are worth the disadvantages? Is this the best alternative?

3. The children

How will my initiating this action affect my relationship with my children? How will they respond to the outcome if I win? If I lose? When and how do I tell the children about the action? How much do I share? How do the children feel about the problem?

Once the decision has been made to take legal action, retain a good, Christian attorney. One reason for this is to have someone who understands your Christian values. For example, a Christian mother may not want her children visiting her ex-spouse who is now living with a new sexual partner without benefit of marriage. However, a judge will often discount those objections, as long as overt sexual activities (even homosexual) are confined to the privacy of the couple's bedroom!

Noncustodial parents who are heavy consumers of alcohol or who are into drugs will not automatically be denied visitation rights. But the court can (and often will) order abstinence during visitation.

A Christian attorney, because of personal acceptance of Christian values, can help a parent to understand the laws and to seek every legal protection possible for the children.

Finding the Right Attorney

When is an attorney needed? Usually when a court decision is involved. In some states a couple who are splitting up peacefully can "do their own divorce" and represent themselves in court. But in any legal situation where the parties are in conflict, attorneys are needed.

The yellow pages of the telephone directory are very helpful for finding plumbers, repair persons, or locksmiths. But choosing an attorney should involve more than random telephoning. Referrals are more reliable. Most pastors know attorneys who have successfully handled similar cases for other church members. Other people in steprelationships may be good referral sources. Or counselors and therapists are usually familiar with attorneys who specialize in family law and have a good reputation.

The best attorney in the world cannot effectively represent a client who is not completely open and honest about facts and feelings. Often clients fail to reveal information they fear would be detrimental to their cases. But truth has a way of surfacing, and an attorney who knows all of the facts will be prepared to effectively respond to all of the issues.

Chapter Twelve
Taking One Step at a Time

And so we come to the end of a book that covers hundreds of concepts, mentions dozens of problems, and gives no guarantees! There are no perfect solutions! Only comforts and encouragements. What works for Sue and Norman doesn't work for Chris and Kay. What is a terrific success in one situation fails miserably in another. In fact, the question remains—what is success or failure in a steprelationship?

When Are You a Success?

—When you have learned to communicate? to discipline? to avoid ulcers?

—When you have launched the stepchildren into their own, independent lives?

—When the marriage has survived in spite of all of the problems?

—When a stepchild impulsively gives a hug and whispers "I love you!"?

—When your spouse assures you that you are a good parent?

—When you feel good?

—When?

When Have You Failed?

On the other hand, when has one failed as a stepparent?

—When the stepchild runs away from home? gets into trouble?

—When the marriage fails?

—When other people criticize the way you relate to the stepchildren?

—When your stepchild yells in anger, "I hate you!"?
—When you feel depressed, angry, or discouraged?
—When?

The truth is there are no set criteria for determining the success or failure of a person in the stepparent role. People develop their own standards for success. When their standards are achieved, people feel successful. And when they fall short of their expectations, people feel that they have failed. Therefore, people who set unrealistic goals must either lower their expectations or consider themselves to have failed. Sometimes the steprelationship doesn't work out in spite of the best efforts of all concerned. In those cases, the people must remember that failure as a stepparent (stepchild or spouse) is not failure as a person!

Encouragements

People struggling in steprelationships need to be affirmed and encouraged to keep going on and on. Key concepts to remember include the following:

1. Keep Christ in the center.

Christ belongs in the center of the family life. When Christ is given His proper place in their lives, people tap into His strength and become powerful enough to overcome life's problems. Under His guidance people find they can navigate the uncharted waters of stepparenthood with confidence. Sometimes like Peter they can even walk on water! Yet, just as Peter did, people can sink if they take their eyes off Jesus and focus on their problems instead.

2. Believe things will work out.

God has promised that all things work together for good in our lives (Romans 8:28). As we read through the Bible, we see that God has been able to turn some pretty unlikely situations into positive experiences. Remember Joseph sold into slavery and later saving his family during the famine? Remember Daniel in the lion's den? David and Goliath? Is a steprelationship too great a challenge for God? No way!

During difficult times, people will want to read and reread the promises in God's Word that will reassure them that with His help they can succeed. Verses such as:

". . . with God all things are possible." (Matthew 19:26)

"I can do all things through Christ which strengtheneth me." (Philippians 4:13)

". . . and as thy days, so shall thy strength be." (Deuteronomy 33:25)

"When thou passest through the waters, I will be with thee; and through the rivers, they shall not overflow thee: when thou walkest through the fire, thou shalt not be burned; neither shall the flame kindle upon thee, For I am the Lord thy God." (Isaiah 43:2-3a)

"If ye abide in Me, and My words abide in you, ye shall ask what ye will, and it shall be done unto you." (John 15:7)

3. Have realistic expectations.

Life is a series of peak and valley experiences. The good times don't last forever, but ("Thank You, Lord!") neither do the bad times. Expecting life to be always easy and pleasant is obviously unrealistic, yet so often people seem so startled when troubles come their way.

People must be accepted as they are—a combination of shortcomings and positive characteristics. Expecting family members to be always kind and loving is unrealistic.

When the steprelationships seem to be always less than what people expect, they may need to take a look at just what is being expected from the relationships, because the expectations may be unrealistic.

4. Recognize the early warning signs of stress overload.

Developing an awareness of when they are operating on reserve energy helps people to be able to take corrective action to reduce their stress levels before they become seriously ill. Taking the time to relax, to regroup, and to gather strength is a real necessity in today's busy world. However, many people don't take time out for regrouping but just plunge on ahead until they wear out. They are like the Israelites who often thought they could conquer their world in their own strength. But the Israelites were admonished in Isaiah 30:15: ". . . in returning and rest shall ye be saved; in quietness and in confidence shall be your strength. . . ."

5. Give the steprelationship time to develop.

Biological families grow slowly. A young man and woman start dating; they get to know each other. Next they are engaged, and then married. Various levels of intimacy are explored and shared: social, recreational, mental, emotional, psychological, spiritual, and physical. They learn to live together. Before a new person—a child—is added to the intimate family unit, the prospective parents have nine months to anticipate and prepare for the change. Any new family members are usually born one at a time, and at least nine months apart, although two or three years is the norm. Integrating new family members into the existing structure is a slow process.

Stepfamilies are significantly different. The couple's courtship and early days of marriage already include children—all of them, all at once. People are expected to develop an intimate relationship with a group of virtual strangers! A new stepparent cannot just concentrate on getting to know one child at a time and ignore the others! And so stepfamily members learn to adjust to each other all at the same time. Over the years family members will relate to each other on varying levels of intimacy, depending on how much of themselves they are willing to risk investing.

Emotional "Economics"

Investing is a key word, as counselor Richard Baker talks of "emotional economics" and how it parallels the financial economy. Much like the person who invests money in the stock market and awaits the returns, closely watching the trends and often reevaluating how the money is invested, people must select carefully how to invest their emotional resources.

Sometimes the rewards are immediate. People love their spouses and are loved in return.

On other transactions the returns are slower in coming. Loving and caring for children and stepchildren is a long-term investment during which a positive outcome sometimes seems dubious.

People cannot invest 100 percent of their resources in only one "stock." For example, children. We would all like to raise well-behaved, healthy children who excel in school, cheerfully volunteer to assist in household chores, relate well with others, are independent and responsible, and who consider us wonderful parents. Maybe we could do just that if both we and the children spent 100 percent of our emotional, mental, and physical resources in achieving those goals. But we have other activities and relationships that claim our attention: careers, friends, education, recreation, church work, personal growth, and relationships with spouses. And so we allocate our resources in priority order and settle for realistic expectations. We give less than 100 percent of ourselves to our roles as parents and understand that the children will be reasonably healthy and well-behaved some of the time. They will seldom do chores without reminding us of child labor laws, and once in a while they'll give us hugs and whisper, "You're not so bad as a parent!"

Unfortunately, some people don't consider the relationship between the investment and the outcome. They invest 10 percent in a project, and expect 100 percent return. It doesn't work that way. A 10 percent investment is more likely to yield a 10—15 percent of ideal return.

When people recognize that the return parallels the investment, they will recognize that concentrating on three or four major goals is preferable to trying to juggle 20 projects. The four goals can have roughly 25 percent of the resources, while the 20 projects would most likely only have about a five percent share. A five percent return is not often worthwhile.

Translated into the stepfamily, emotional economics work best when the members focus on two or three areas of growing together and let the lower priority changes wait their turns.

People are always reconsidering their investments. Is this stock paying off? Would another stock be more worthwhile? Emotional investments ought also to be reevaluated. Is this how one really wants to invest himself? As the variables change, so should the decision about the investment. Inflexibility more often than not results in a failure to achieve any of the desired outcomes.

But perhaps the saddest people are those who hoard their emotional resources without investing, because the fear of losing makes risking impossible. They have their own strength—and self-sufficiency. And their own loneliness! They interact superficially, almost perfunctorily. They marry, have children, and move through life without ever interacting on an intimate personal level. They neither give generously, not receive liberally, for only as people invest can they multiply their resources.

Investments are risky. They may fail—or succeed. But

without risk no financial fortunes have been made. And no one ever lives fully, richly, or abundantly without investing emotionally in life! And that includes people in stepfamilies.

One Step at a Time

People living together in step will feel more successful if they acknowledge that they must learn to set realistic goals for the family and to accept the frail humanity of each other. As they jointly invest in the relationship, a strong family unity slowly forms, binding the members together. The investments begin to pay off, and some progress toward the goals becomes visible. But not too quickly.

In fact, the secret of succeeding as a stepfamily is taking things one step at a time!

Appendix A
Resources for Stepfamilies

When the problem is child abuse, the following organizations may provide referral assistance, without contacting the police authorities:

American Human Association
5351 South Roslyn
Englewood, CO 80110
(303) 779-1400

Parents Anonymous
Dept. RB, Box F
2810 Artesia Blvd.
Redondo Beach, CA 90278
(213) 371-3501

If you are looking for assistance for steprelationships, the specific resources are still quite few. However, check the index to the yellow pages of your local telephone book for such listings as:

—Organizations for women
—Organizations for men
—Organizations for families
—Organizations for stepfamilies
—Counseling services
—Social service agencies
     (child abuse, spouse abuse, counseling assistance)
—Legal Aid Society—Domestic Relations Unit
—Parents' Anonymous

Or write to those listed below for information.

When the issue is rights for the natural father, contact:

Equal Rights for Fathers
P.O. Box 6327
Albany, CA 94706
(415) 848-2323

For information about help for stepfamilies or how to start your own chapter, contact:

Stepfamily Association of America
900 Welch Rd.
Palo Alto, CA 94304
(415) 328-0723

Stepfamily Foundation of California, Inc.
39 E. Main, #2
Los Gatos, CA 95030
(408) 354-2900

To be referred to a reputable counselor, the following associations are recommended:

American Association of Marriage and Family Counselors
225 Yale Avenue
Claremont, CA 91711

Association of Family Conciliation Courts
10015 S.W. Terwillinger Blvd.
Portland, OR 97219
(503) 244-1181

Appendix B
Bibliography

Augsburger, David. Caring Enough to Confront. Glendale, CA: Regal Books, 1977.

Bach, George and Peter Wyden. The Intimate Enemy. New York: William Morrow & Co., 1968.

Baer, Jean. The Second Wife. New York: Doubleday and Co., 1972.

Bergler, Edmund. Divorce Won't Help. New York: Hart, 1948.

Berkowitz, Bernard. "Legal Incidents of Today's 'Step' Relationship: 'Cinderella' Revisited." Family Law Quarterly (September 1970) 4:209—29.

Bernard, Jessie. "Remarriage of the Widowed and the Divorced," in Rush S. Cavan, ed., Marriage and the Family in the Modern World. New York: Thomas Y. Crowell, 1960. Pp. 416—24.

Bernard, Jessie Shirley. Remarriage: A Study of Marriage. New York: Russell & Russell, 1971.

Bessell, Harold, Ph.D., and Thomas P. Kelly Jr. The Parent Book. Sacramento, CA: Jalmar Press, 1977.

Biller, Henry, and Dennis Meredith. Father Power. New York: David McKay & Co., Inc., 1974.

Blaine, Graham B., Jr. "The Children of Divorce." Atlantic Monthly (March 1963) 211:98—101.

Bohannon, Paul, ed. Divorce and After. New York: Anchor Books, 1971.

Bowerman, Charles E., and Donald P. Irish. "Some Relationships of Stepchildren to Their Parents." Marriage and Family Living (May 1962) 24:113—21.

Bowerman, Charles E., and Donald P. Irish. "Some Relationships of Stepchildren to Their Parents," in Marriage and Family in the Modern World, edited by Ruth Shonle Cavan. New York: Thomas Y. Crowell, 1969.

Bowlby, John. Attachment and Loss, Vol. II, Separation, Anxiety and Anger. New York: Basic Books, Inc., 1973.

Brothers, Joyce. "Making a Second Marriage Work," Good Housekeeping (February 1972) 174:6.

Burchinal, Lee G. "Characteristics of Adolescents from Unbroken, Broken and Reconstituted Families." Marriage and Family Living (February 1964) 26:44—51.

Caine, Lynn. Widow. New York: William Morrow & Co., 1974.

Despert, J. Louise. Children of Divorce. New York: Doubleday and Company, 1953.

Duberman, Lucille. Marriage and Its Alternatives. New York: Praeger Publishers, 1974.

Duberman, Lucille. The Reconstituted Family: A Study of Remarried Couples and Their Children. Chicago: Nelson-Hall Publishers, 1975.

Durkheim, Emil, and A. Ellis. Incest: The Nature and Origin of the Taboo. Trans. and Introduction by Edward Saragin. New York: Lyle Stuart, 1963.

Dyer, Wayne W. Your Erroneous Zones. New York: Avon, 1976.

Epstein, Joseph. Divorced in America: Marriage in an Age of Possibility. New York: E. P. Dutton & Co., 1974.

Fairfield, James G. T. When You Don't Agree. Scottdale, PA: Herald Press, 1977.

Fast, Irene, and Albert Cain. "The Stepparent Role—Potential for Disturbance in Family Functioning." American Journal of Orthopsychiatry. No. 36 (1966):489—96.

Gardner, Richard A. The Boys and Girls Book About Divorce. New York: Science House, 1970.

Gaulke, Earl H. You Can Have a Family Where Everybody Wins. St. Louis: Concordia Publishing House, 1975.

Ginott, Haim G. Between Parent and Child. New York: Avon, 1969.

Ginott, Haim G. Between Parent and Teenager. New York: Macmillan Company, 1969.

Goldstein, Joseph, Anna Freud, and Albert J. Solnit. Beyond the Best Interests of the Child. New York: Free Press, 1971.

Goode, William. After Divorce. Glencoe, IL: Free Press, 1956.

Gordon, Thomas. Parent Effectiveness Training. New York: Peter H. Wyden, Inc., 1970.

Grollman, Earl A. Talking About Death: A Dialogue Between Parent and Child. Boston: Beacon Press, 1970.

Hancock, Maxine. People in Progress. Old Tappan, NJ: Fleming H. Revell Company, 1978.

Heim, Pamela. The Art of Married Love. Irvine, CA: Harvest House Publishers, 1978.

Hill, Archie. Closed World of Love. New York: Simon and Schuster, 1976.

Hunt, Morton M. The World of the Formerly Married. New York: McGraw-Hill Book Company, 1966.

Johnson, Rex. Communication, Key to Your Parents. Irvine, CA: Harvest House Publishers, 1978.

Klein, Carol. The Single Parent Experience. New York: Avon, 1973.

Krantzler, Mel. Creative Divorce. New York: M. Evans & Co., 1974.

LaHaye, Beverly. How to Develop Your Child's Temperament. Irvine, CA: Harvest House Publishers, 1977.

LaHaye, Tim. How to Be Happy Though Married. Wheaton, IL: Tyndale House Publishers, 1968.

LaHaye, Tim, and Beverly LaHaye. Spirit Controlled Family Living. Old Tappan, NJ: Fleming H. Revell Company, 1978.

Lofas, Jeannette, and Ruth Roosevelt. Living in Step. New York: Stein & Day, 1976.

Lowe, Patricia Tracey. The Cruel Stepmother. Englewood Cliffs, NJ: Prentice-Hall, 1970.

Maddox, Brenda. The Half-Parent. New York: M. Evans & Co., 1975.

Mayleas, Davidyne. Rewedded Bliss. New York: Basic Books, Inc., 1977.

Meriam, Adele Stuart. The Stepfather in the Family. Chicago: University of Chicago Press, 1940.

Noble, June, and William Noble. The Custody Trap. New York: Hawthorn Books, 1975.

Noble, June, and William Noble. How to Live with Other People's Children. New York: Hawthorn Books, 1977.

Perry, Joseph B., and Edwin H. Pfuhl Jr. "Adjustments of Children in 'Solo' and 'Remarriage' Homes," Marriage and Family Living (May 1963) 25:221—223.

Podolsky, Edward. "The Emotional Problems of the Stepchild." Mental Hygiene, No. 39 (1855):49—53.

Poussaint, A. A. "Are Second Marriages Better?" Ebony Magazine (March 1975) 30:55—56.

McRoberts, Darlene. Second Marriage. Minneapolis: Augsburg Publishing House, 1978.

Roosevelt, Ruth, and Jeannette Lofas. Living in Step. New York: McGraw-Hill, 1977.

Rosenbaum, Jean. Becoming Yourself: The Teen Years. Cincinnati: St. Anthony Messenger Press, 1970.

Rosenbaum, Jean and Veryl Rosenbaum. Stepparenting. Corte Madera, CA: Chandler & Sharp Publishers, Inc., 1977.

Rydman, E.J. "Advice to Second Wives." Harper's Bazaar (April 1973) 106: 104—105.

Salk, Lee. "You and Your Stepchildren." Harper's Bazaar (June 1975) 108:81.

Satir, Virginia. Conjoint Family Therapy. Palo Alto, CA: Science and Behavior Books, Inc., 1967, revised ed.

Schulman, Gerda. "Myths That Intrude on the Adaptation of the Stepfamily." Social Casework, No. 53 (1972) :131—39.

Schwartz, Anne C. "Reflections on Divorce and Remarriage." Social Casework, No. 49 (1968) :213—17.

Simon, Anne W. Stepchild in the Family. New York: The Odyssey Press, 1964.

Smith, William. The Stepchild. Chicago: University of Chicago Press, 1953.

Smoke, Jim. Growing Through Divorce. Irvine, CA: Harvest House Publishers, 1976.

Sponn, Owen, and Nancie Sponn. Your Child? I Thought It Was My Child! Pasadena, CA: Ward Richie Press, 1977.

Spock, Benjamin, M.D. Problems of Parents. Boston: Houghton Mifflin Co., 1962.

Spock, Benjamin, M.D. Raising Children in a Difficult Time. New York: W. W. Norton, 1974.

Stark, G. U. "Seven on a Honeymoon." Parents Magazine (May 1971) 46:445.

Steinzor, Bernard. When Parents Divorce: A New Approach to New Relationships. New York: Pantheon Books, 1969.

Stern, Bernard J. The Family, Past and Present. New York: Appleton-Century, 1935.

Stoop, Dave, and Jan Stoop. The Total(ed) Parent. Irvine, CA: Harvest House Publishers, 1978.

Stuart, Irving R., and Lawrence E. Abt, eds. Children of Separation and Divorce. New York: Grossman Publishers, 1972.

Thomson, Helen. The Successful Stepparent. New York: Harper and Row, 1966.

Visher, Emily B., and John S. Visher. Stepfamilies. New York: Brunner/Mazel, 1979.

Wanderer, Zev, and Tracy Cabot. Letting Go. New York: G. P. Putnam's Sons, 1978.

Wilt, Joy. Super-Parent. Waco, TX: Ward Books, 1977.

Wise, Robert L. Your Churning Place. Glendale, CA: Regal Books, 1977.

Wright, Norman. An Answer to Family Communication. Irvine, CA: Harvest House Publishers, 1977.

Wright, Norman, and Marvin Inmone. Dating, Waiting and Choosing a Mate. Irvine, CA: Harvest House Publishers, 1978.

Wright, Norman, and Rex Johnson. Communication, Key to Your Teens. Ivine, CA: Harvest House Publishers, 1978.